FENCING

FENCING

Techniques of Foil, Épée and Sabre

Brian Pitman

The Crowood Press

First published in 1988 by
The Crowood Press
Ramsbury, Marlborough,
Wiltshire SN8 2HE

British Library Cataloguing in Publication Data

Pitman, Brian
   Fencing: techniques of foil, epee and
   sabre.
   1. Sports: Fencing – Manuals
   I. Title
   796.8'6

ISBN 1 85223 152 1

Picture credits:

Figs 2 and 54 by Karina Hoskyns;
Figs 17, 26 and 56 by Peter Barratt;
Fig 53 by Gareth Everett;
Fig 81 by Alex Yeung;
all demonstration photographs by Tony Bowran.

Typeset by Columns of Reading
Printed in Great Britain at the University Printing House, Oxford

Contents

Foreword

With this book Brian Pitman has contributed a much-needed addition to the fencing library, an up-to-date manual of the sport.

After a brief introduction and historical review, the author provides comprehensive instruction on a wide range of strokes and movements at all three weapons, foil, épée and sabre, as well as offering a solid grounding in the basic elements common to all three.

This is very much the practical book a manual should be. Descriptions are followed by instructions for practice and check lists of what to concentrate on, and the text is supported by a very full set of photographs and diagrams. It offers a wealth of technical guidance and support to those involved in coaching the sport. At the same time it caters for any fencer, from the beginner to the intermediate, who wants to supplement or reinforce the work of his coach, for example by practising at home.

Brian Pitman is well qualified to be the author of such a book. He has been national coach to the Amateur Fencing Association since 1981. Through his travels in that role at home and abroad, his contacts with foreign senior fencing coaches and his work with the technical committee of the Académie d'Armes Internationale, he has had every opportunity to keep abreast of the latest ideas. He is a member of the National Coaching Foundation's South-Eastern Region Steering Committee.

He continues to teach at all levels, from small children to full international fencers, and is the senior coach at the largest fencing club in the country, the London Thames Fencing Club. He has competitive experience at all three weapons both as an amateur and, more recently, representing Great Britain on three occasions in the Fencing Masters' World Championships.

Peter Jacobs
Vice-President, Amateur Fencing Association

Preface

I have written this book for the enquiring fencer, from beginner to intermediate standard. It will supplement the coaching he or she may receive from his or her own coach or master and help with terminology and the acquisition of skills. The aspiring fencer needs to glean as much information as possible in a short time; waiting for the next lesson is like waiting a year. With this book, you can use the time in between your fencing lessons to learn more about the strokes you are using and their tactical application.

In my early days of fencing I found it difficult to get to a club, let alone a coach. I would spend many a happy hour with a textbook in hand, practising opposite a mirror, imitating the illustrations in the book. I hope this book can be used effectively in this way. I hope that coaches will also find new ideas within its pages, and a lot of technical information to help them in their training.

I have often been asked how to coach left-handed fencers; many fencers and coaches get confused about the lines and positions of the left-hander. The left-hander is a mirror image of the right-hander and lines are named according to the sword arm and by right or left. I hope that the many photo-graphs of left-handed fencers included in this book will dispel confusion.

I was introduced to fencing by an AFA coach, Henry Liddle, and further encouraged and enthused by such people as Peter March, another amateur coach. Later I was influenced by my old friend and fencing master, Bill Harmer Brown, and, through National Training, the late Roger Crosnier and Bob Anderson, two former national coaches. Steve Boston also developed and strengthened my sabre and I have tried to remain loyal to all these people and their teaching. From the knowledge and expertise they gave me, I have pursued researches on my own account, exchanging ideas and information with masters all over the world. That spark encouraged so many years ago lit the way for even more progressive thinking and, although the solid technical foundation was there, I have been able to build on that and develop my own ideas and be my own man, never forgetting what I owe to those dedicated people.

This book could not have been produced without my wife, who has supported me throughout my career and who has been responsible for the preparation of the manuscript. To her my grateful thanks.

Lastly, I salute you, the fencer.

Brian Pitman

PART ONE
ALL WEAPONS

1 The History of Fencing

Single combat has existed since man first appeared on this planet. Early man had to hunt for his food and be ready to fight to hold on to his possessions and he used the same weapons for single combat as he did for hunting. The development of weapons from the early clubs to the sword varied according to country and culture. Swords started out as large, two-handed weapons but, with successive improvements in the quality of steel, they gradually became thinner and lighter, finally evolving into the single-handed weapons with thin, flexible blades we know today.

Whilst in Britain the favoured sword was a cutting weapon, in Italy a pointed weapon was preferred. Since Italy was one of the centres of culture, these weapons gradually swept across the continent. English swordsmen were inclined to be suspicious of these weapons and contemptuous of their points, and when the early fencing masters came from Italy during the fifteenth and sixteenth centuries, they found it very difficult to establish themselves.

This was the era of prize fighting. Junior masters (or provosts) gained their qualifications by fighting for a prize before their peers and they were obliged to demonstrate many weapons from single stick through to the cutting blades and then on to the points. When the first Italian masters arrived they

Fig 1   Taken from the seventeenth-century manuscript *Recueil de Planche sur les Sciences et les Arts – Escrime* by Angelo – a treatise detailing all the different movements and skills involved in fencing.

10

found themselves having to prove the value of the points against the cutting edge. Some did not survive.

J.D. Aylward in his book *The English Master of Arms* says that 'during the fifteenth and sixteenth centuries a surprising number of Italians faced the hardship of a journey to England. A few made it their adopted country, others went back to their native land after a more or less profitable stay.'

As the fencing masters formed themselves into guilds their teaching became much more technical, and technique and tactics – along with the most modern equipment of the time – were paramount. They still form the basis of modern fencing. For practice a weapon known as a foil was used, with a button placed on the point for safety. The button was large enough to protect the eye, which had hitherto been very vulnerable. Nevertheless, the weapon was still quite dangerous, a hit in the face or neck could cause considerable injury and the edges of the blades became serrated through constant use and could cut the arms, neck and legs. The target was therefore limited to an area which could be padded – the torso. This is still the target used in foil fencing today.

The other great danger was that if two combatants, whilst practising, attacked simultaneously the blades, uncontrolled, might go anywhere. It therefore became necessary to define a 'right of way', which was given to the person initiating the attack. This, which was introduced as a gentlemen's agreement, has now become a rule, known as a 'convention'. Once masks were re-introduced in the mid-nineteenth century (there *are* records of masks having been used in Ancient Egypt), the size of the button was reduced. Fencers started to wear specially designed jackets but the conventions remained the same.

Occasional duels were still being fought, although they were now against the law in many countries. The weapon used for these was a much larger one, the épée. Obviously, in a duel it matters not where the opponent is hit, so the whole body was the target. Fencers who were practising purely for sporting purposes decided that they would like to try this form of combat, so the épée was introduced as a fencing weapon, with a button on the end, the whole body the target and no rights of way.

The cutting-edge weapon was still being used as a weapon of war in the form of the naval cutlass and the cavalry sabre. Gradually these were developed into another sporting weapon, the sabre. The conventions were kept as for the foil but the target was changed to the area above the waist. So today we have three weapons in modern fencing, the foil, the épée and the sabre, much changed from the days of their original conception.

2 Aims of the Game

Fencing takes place on a specially marked out strip (or piste) and a bout, or fight, consists of two fencers in a combative situation, each trying to score a set number of hits in order to win. Whether a hit is valid (scores) depends on the weapon: with the foil and épée hits are made with the point, whereas with the sabre hits are scored by cutting with the blade as well as hitting with the point and each of the three weapons has a different target. A bout is conducted by a president or referee who awards the hits as they occur, according to the conventions, and interprets and applies the rules. The first fencer who scores the required number of hits (usually five) is the winner of the bout. There is a time limit for the fencing in each bout.

In competitions competitors are grouped in pools, usually groups of six. The fencers in

Fig 2   Ladies' Team Foil Championships, 1987 – Hungary versus Romania.

each pool fight one another and those with the best results are promoted to the next round. At least half the pool must be promoted, the lower half being eliminated from the competition. When each round of pools is drawn up the fencers are seeded according to their results in the previous round. As the competition develops, the match plan may change to direct elimination, in which case the number of hits being fought for is increased: for men, the first to reach ten hits wins; for women, the first to reach eight.

To fence competitively, one must be athletic, quick-witted, and agile in mind and body. A high degree of skill is required. The bout consists of bluff and counter-bluff, feeding false information to one's opponent while trying to anticipate his or her next move. It demands great concentration and totally absorbs the mind. Thus fencing provides good physical exercise, employing prac-tically every muscle, while relieving stressful tensions and acting as a tonic to the mind as well as the body.

The need for co-ordination, concentration, self-discipline and control of the emotions make fencing especially beneficial to young people as an education for life. The social aspects of the sport should never be dis-regarded; it is equally appealing to men and to women and to all ages and abilities.

Fencing has been an Olympic sport since the inauguration of the modern Olympics. Except in Olympic years, world champion-ships and world youth championships are held annually. The world governing body is the Fédération Internationale d'Escrime (FIE), to which the British governing body, the Amateur Fencing Association (The de Beaumont Centre, 83 Perham Road, London W14 9SP) is affiliated. The Schools Fencing Union regulates the national age-group com-petitions for schoolchildren.

3 Basic Skills

Certain basic movements and positions in fencing are common to all three weapons so, irrespective of which weapon you prefer, you are well advised to practise these until they become trained reactions.

What is the best way to learn new movements? Fencing movements need a high degree of co-ordination. This means that the brain must learn them as a whole, and not in isolated pieces. Movements may be split up into progressions in the initial stages of learning but should never be isolated so that they lose their rhythm. The whole movements become habit patterns and the best way to learn these is to visualise what it is you want to do. Try to create this picture with actual movement and then – most important – analyse the movement, compare it with your original picture, revisualise and correct it in the light of your performance. Keep doing this until you are satisfied. If you do not have a coach a lot of early practice can be done in front of a mirror.

THE ON GUARD POSITION

Balance is important in all sports but particularly so in combat sports such as fencing. When balance is lost, the ability to move arms and legs independently of one another is impossible and the resulting instability renders the fencer unable to defend or attack. The lower you can get your centre of gravity, the more stable you are and the less likely to fall over.

To be on guard is to be ready and this is an attitude of mind as well as of body. I draw a parallel with a workman who, when beginning a job, first rolls up his sleeves.

Place your feet at right angles, with the leading foot (right for a right-hander, left for a left-hander) at the distance of an ordinary walking pace (two foot lengths) from the rear foot. An imaginary line should run through your back and front heels and your opponent's front and back heels. This is shown in the photographs and is known as the 'line of fence'.

The trunk should be turned three-quarters to the front. The front arm, the sword arm, should be bent and raised until the hand is breast high and the elbow approximately a sword-arm position for foil and épée. The sword arm position for foil and épée. The back arm should be raised, bent at the

Fig 3   The on guard position – note the position of the feet and the line of fence. The trunk is upright and the knees are well bent.

elbow, fingers relaxed and level with the eyes, forming a V from the shoulder. Make sure that your shoulders are level and your head and neck relaxed and facing towards the opponent. Then bend both your knees so that the weight of your body is between your feet.

Check List
- The feet should be at right angles.
- The hips are three-quarters to the front.

- The knees must be evenly bent (make sure that the weight is not on one leg).
- The front and back arms are bent to the correct positions and relaxed.
- Shoulders, head and neck are relaxed.

PREPARATION AND FITNESS

As fencing is a physical sport as well as a brain game, it is best to prepare oneself

Fig 4 Koppang, winner of the World Youth Épée Championship for the second time. Note the almost classic on guard position in the middle of a bout. Experienced fencers vary the position and height of their rear arm, but beginners should start with the position described on page 14.

before fencing by doing a few simple exercises to stretch the muscles to their fullest extent, especially those of the hips and legs. Fencing is a dynamic activity and training should be done at speed. This is why it is very important to stretch the muscles first. Apart from sprinting, which is good for most sports, training should be based on actual fencing movements to build up the power in the appropriate muscles and so provide the energy necessary for competition fencing. You should use all your available time at the club in free play with as many different fencers as possible. The physical demands of fencing are very great, and greatest on the legs, so it is important to start all training or competition sessions with the stretching and flexibility exercises suggested below. Change the exercises at regular intervals to keep them fresh and interesting. Any good fencing master or coach will be only too pleased to help with any new ideas.

Exercises

Feet and Ankles

The importance of exercising the feet is often overlooked by athletes.

a) Stand barefoot with your feet flat on the floor, draw up the toes, then straighten them, working each foot in turn.
b) Raise yourself up on your toes and then lower your heels. Repeat several times.
c) Stand with your feet slightly apart. Now walk forwards on the sides of your feet, keeping balance. Place your feet flat, then repeat.
d) Stand, holding a support with one hand, with your feet together and your toes pointing to the front, with legs straight. Lift one foot from the ground and circle it several times, first one way then the other. Repeat the exercise with the other foot.

Calf Muscles

a) Stand with one foot half a pace in front of the other, toes to the front. Keeping the back heel on the ground, bend the front knee over the front foot, gradually deepening the bend. Change feet and repeat.

Upper Leg Muscles

a) To stretch the front thigh muscles (the quadriceps), kneel upright and lean back until you can touch the ground behind you.
b) To stretch the back thigh muscles (the hamstrings), sit on the ground, straighten your right leg and tuck your left leg underneath your right thigh. Incline your upper body towards your leg (it is not necessary to touch your leg with your head). Change legs and repeat.
c) In a squatting position, extend your right leg to the side with the side of the foot on the ground. With your hands on your hips, bend from the waist towards extended leg. Change legs and repeat.
d) Holding on to a support with one hand, stand with feet together and legs straight. Swing one foot in front of you, toe pointing, as high as you can. Lower to the floor. Now swing it backwards as far as possible, keeping the knee straight. Replace. Now raise the leg as far as possible to the side and replace. Having done this several times, circle the leg through these three positions, then reverse. Change legs and repeat several times.

Upper Body Flexing and Stretching

a) Stand with your back to a wall, your feet apart and slightly away from it. Keep your feet still but twist your body from the hips until you can touch the wall behind you with both hands. Return to

Fig 5   Walk forwards on the sides of your feet.

Fig 8   Stretch abductors and adductors.

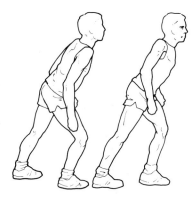

Fig 6   With your rear heel on the ground, stretch the calf muscle. Repeat with other leg.

Fig 9   Stretch the back thigh muscles.

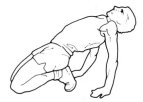

Fig 7   Stretch the front thigh muscles.

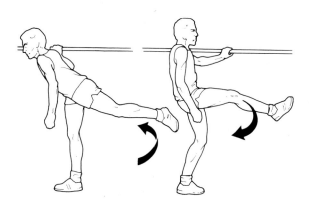

Fig 10   Hip flexing – circle the left leg from the hip. Repeat with the right leg.

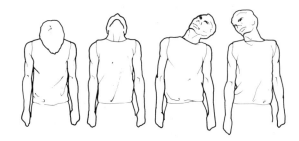

Fig 13   Flexing the neck. Lower your head forwards, your chin touching your chest. Tip your head back as far as possible. Lower your head to one side. Lower your head to the opposite side.

Fig 11   Upper body flexing. Twist and touch the wall behind with both hands. Repeat in the opposite direction. Straighten your back and raise your hands above your head. Bend and touch the floor beneath your feet.

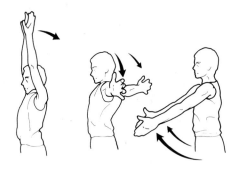

Fig 12   Circling both arms, flexing the shoulders.

the first position and repeat the exercise in the opposite direction. Return to centre. Straighten your back, raise your hands above your head and reach up as high as you can. Bend and touch the floor between your feet. Lift your arms back up high, straightening your back. Keeping the back straight, lower your arms, then repeat the whole exercise.

Shoulders

a)   Stand with legs apart. Start circling one arm, keeping as wide a circle as possible, forwards, up, round to the back, and back to its original position. Then circle the other arm in the same way. Now circle both arms together, brushing your ears with the insides of your arms as you go. Finally, repeat the exercise, circling your arms in the opposite direction.

b)   Stand with your feet apart, arms bent across the chest, fingertips touching, elbows in line with your shoulders. Pull your elbows back as far as you can, parting your hands as you do so. Return to the original position and consciously relax your shoulders. Repeat this several times.

Neck

a) Standing upright, with your hands by your sides, lower your head forwards until your chin touches your chest. Raise your head and now tip it back as far as you can with your chin up in the air. Return your head to the central position. Now lower it to one side, back to the centre, and then to the other side and back to the centre. Repeat several times. Do not circle the head as this is not a good exercise.

All these stretching and flexibility exercises should be done slowly, gradually stretching and flexing the joints. Having completed the movements relax the muscles and joints by jogging gently round a room or on the spot, consciously shaking your limbs to release the tensions built up by the exercises.

Fitness for fencing is achieved by doing exercises which duplicate the movements required in the fight situation, so, in the absence of a fencing coach, the best way to improve your fitness is to do footwork, including lunges, flèches, etc. You should set yourself one minute of solid work, without a break. As you get fitter, increase the number of repetitions with short recovery breaks in between. Try to achieve as much speed as possible whilst retaining the skill factor of the movement. Beware of substituting speed for skill.

MOVEMENT AND DISTANCE

In the early days of swordsmanship, there was very little movement backwards and forwards. The contestants would circle one another, seeking out a weakness, rather like boxers. When they closed the distance to attack, they needed wrestling skills as well as those of a swordsman. Like animals defending their ground, to go backwards was to give way. This gradually altered – probably because of the change of weapons – until one of the last known duels had to be abandoned when both combatants developed blisters on their hands!

Modern fencing does not allow wrestling or the use of the unarmed hand, and bouts are now fought on a strip of ground called a piste. It is therefore important for fencers to be able to move backwards as well as forwards. Furthermore, the type or combination of the footwork to be used is determined by the fencer's judgement of the best way to cover the distance necessary to be able to hit his opponent.

Stepping Forwards and Backwards

A step forwards in fencing is made with both feet. To step forwards, first raise the front toe slightly and move the front foot forwards, landing heel first. Then clear the rear foot from the ground and move it forwards to its original distance from the front foot, landing with the ball of the foot first. The 'on guard' position of the body – with knees bent and at right angles – is maintained throughout the movement. At no time do the feet cross.

To step backwards the procedure is reversed. The back foot is moved first, landing on the ball of the foot. The front foot follows and lands heel first.

Do both of these movements slowly at first, then in different combinations: two steps forwards, one back; three steps forwards, two back; three steps backwards, two forwards, and so on. Gradually speed up, keeping the rhythm, until your steps forwards and backwards are fast and light and the lifting of the toe is smooth and relaxed.

Check List
- Maintain the on guard position properly throughout.
- Check that your weight is between your feet.
- Keep your knees bent.

- Don't close the gap between the feet.
- Keep your head still and central, as failure to do so could make you lose balance.
- Practise moving the arms independently of the legs.

The Lunge and Recovery

A fencer can, and often does, just step forward, straightening the arm to hit his opponent, but the risk is that in so doing he will impale himself on the opposing point or that the opponent will attack in the middle of the step. A safer way of delivering an attack and one that is used by all fencers, is to lunge with the sword and then recover back to the on guard position. Study the photographs of the lunge. If you can ask someone to watch you or, better still, practise the following set of movements in front of a mirror, it will help.

The stages of the lunge

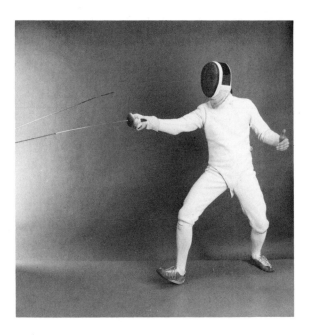

Fig 15 Keeping the rear foot flat, clear the front foot from the ground a mere couple of centimetres or so.

Fig 14 Starting from the on guard position, the point leading.

Fig 16 The final position of the lunge. Keep the shoulders and arms relaxed.

The whole movement must start with the point (for foil and épée) or the cutting edge (for sabre) being thrust forwards. This is necessary to comply with the conventions and give you the right of way; it also provides as much cover as possible from the guard and helps with accuracy and smoothness, making the movement difficult to detect from the outset.

Straighten the sword arm at shoulder height, no higher, with the thumb uppermost. Do not lock the elbow as this will not only cause tension in the arm and shoulder but will kill the feel of the blade in your fingers and make it very difficult to respond easily and efficiently to a changing situation.

Having practised this, combine it with a step forwards. Move the hand forward just before moving the feet by imagining that you have a piece of string linking your wrist and front foot. The string is loose but as you straighten the sword arm it becomes taut and pulls the foot; the straighter your arm becomes, the further your front foot travels. The next stage is to repeat this action, this time keeping the back foot still and carrying the front foot further and further forwards until the knee, bent at a right angle, is over the front instep and the foot meets the ground heel first. To do this you must straighten the back leg and, for balance, drop your back arm so that the hand is lightly touching the thigh. The trunk remains upright. This position is known as the 'lunge'. To make it an effective way of delivering an attack, it must be done as fast as possible. When you clear the front foot from the ground, the thrust for the lunge comes from the back leg. If this power is developed correctly, it should be possible to carry the front foot a mere inch or two from the ground to its final position.

There are three types of lunge: the 'explosive lunge', which is very fast and is used when a sudden opening occurs; the 'accelerating lunge', in which power is built up so that the hit is made when travelling at maximum speed (this lunge is useful when executing more than one blade movement); and the 'waiting lunge' in which the fencer makes the lunge last as long as possible in order to discover and deceive the defence.

The recovery is the same for all three and follows immediately upon completion of the attack. Use the spring of the front knee as you land to start the recovery. Push with the heel of the front foot, bending the back knee as you do so, and bring the front foot back to the on guard position. Allow the rear arm to bend back to its original position and, as the front foot hits the ground, heel first, bend your sword arm back to its on guard position.

Check List (lunge)
- The hand and sword arm must precede the foot.
- The foot moves a few inches above ground, landing heel first.
- Straighten the back leg, dropping the rear arm.
- The front knee must be over the front foot, the knee bent at right angles.
- The body must be upright on lunge, in the same position as for the on guard.
- The hips are three-quarters to the front.
- The shoulders are relaxed and both at same height.
- The rear foot should remain flat on ground.

Check List (recovery)
- Raise the front toe and push from the heel while collapsing the back knee.
- Raise the rear arm to its original position.
- Bend the sword arm back to the on guard position.
- Return to the original position between the feet, both at right angles (the front foot travels just above the ground).

Jumping Forwards and Backwards

These jumps are made in order to cover distance fast or change direction suddenly, so they are made across the floor and not upwards. Clear the front foot from the ground and kick it forwards, simultaneously jumping with the back foot so that both feet land together. Going backwards, kick the rear foot back, jumping simultaneously with the front foot, both feet landing together. The distance can be varied according to the need.

The Flèche Attack

'Flèche' means arrow, which describes the shape of this attack. Straighten the sword arm, shifting the weight as you do so, allowing the body to tip forward to as near a horizontal position as possible. As you lean forward and feel yourself overbalancing, let the rear foot swing past the front one. As it does so, push off from the front foot, propelling the body forward, hitting the opponent while the body is flying through the air. The push from the front foot is similar to that of a sprinter exploding from the blocks. The hit must arrive before or not later than when the rear foot hits the floor.

Check List
- The sword hand and arm must precede the foot.
- The shoulders are three-quarters to front.
- Allow enough room to run past your

Fig 17   Left: Jumping backwards – kick the rear foot back.
Right: A flèche attack at épée.

Fig 18   A flèche attack at sabre. Note the angle of the body
through the air (like an arrow).

opponent without touching him after a hit is scored.

- Hit before or as the rear foot touches the ground.
- Choose time and distance carefully.

The Ballestra

This ballestra is a combination of two forms of footwork. It starts with a jump forward, the front foot slightly ahead of the rear one, although both feet land together. The front foot lands on the ball and immediately travels forwards into a lunge. As an alternative, when the front foot lands after the initial jump, instead of moving into a lunge you can move the back foot through to form a flèche.

The lunge executed with a ballestra covers the same distance, at about the same speed, as a lunge performed with a step forwards. The difference is really in the rhythm, and this can catch an opponent unawares.

Practice

Try jumping forwards and, as you do so, beat the floor with the ball of the front foot while the rear foot lands flat. The front foot is then rapidly carried forwards to a half-lunge. Gradually increase this to a full lunge.

Check List
- The action should propel you forwards over the ground. Take care not to jump upwards.
- Both feet should land together, the beat of the front foot triggering the lunge.
- Make the beat with the ball of the foot.

THE SALUTE

It is customary to salute your opponent before a bout and your fencing master before and after a lesson. This courteous custom has been passed down through the centuries.

The salute

Fig 19   The sword held down obliquely.

Fig 20   Raise the sword above the head.

Fig 21 Bring it back to a perpendicular position.

Fig 22 Sweep the sword away to its original position.

With your mask held under the non-sword arm, feet at right angles, heels touching, and your sword held down obliquely to the front, raise the sword above the head at an angle of approximately 45 degrees from the body, bring it back to a perpendicular position, guard in line with the lips, then sweep it away downwards to the original position.

It is also the custom to shake hands after a bout, using the non-sword hand.

SAFETY

As with all sports, the correct equipment and clothing must be used, not only to protect against accidents but to enable you to perform efficiently and effectively. Fencers have the responsibility of arming and equipping themselves and I suggest that you approach one of the equipment suppliers and seek advice about the most suitable equipment for your needs. Before you can actually practise hitting anyone or have them practise actions against yourself, you must have the following items of equipment:

a) A mask in good condition (no rust on the mesh, the bib correctly attached, and strong enough to withstand a hit).
b) A fencing jacket.
c) An underplastron (an undergarment covering the upper part of the sword arm and chest with no seam under the arm).
d) A glove for the sword hand with a gauntlet covering the opening of the sleeve.

If you join a club, it is usually possible for beginners to borrow equipment. If the club is affiliated to the Amateur Fencing Association somebody will be responsible for the equipment, but equipment borrowed from other sources may not have been used for some time, and it would be safer to get a knowledgeable fencer to check it.

A FEW SIMPLE RULES

The following rules are common to all weapons.

a) Never point a weapon at someone who is not wearing a mask.
b) Do not run while holding a weapon by the handle. Always hold it by the point when walking or running.
c) Put your foil down before donning your mask.
d) Ensure that your foil or épée has a covering over the point and that your weapon is not broken near the tip.
e) If you break a blade – as you undoubtedly will some day – dismantle the weapon before putting it away.

PART TWO
THE FOIL

4 Conventions

HITS AND THE TARGET

The foil is a pointed weapon and valid hits may only be scored by hitting the target in such a way that had the point not been covered it would have penetrated. This is called 'hitting with the property of penetration'.

The target is the body, excluding the arms, legs and head – from a line where the sleeve seam crosses the head of the humerus down to and including the V of the groin and a straight line across the top of the hips (ilium).

The target is divided into high line and low line and eight defensive positions. The four

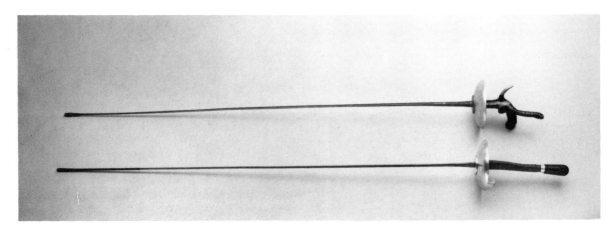

Fig 23   The foil. There are various grips. These are the main two.
Above is a popular form of orthopaedic grip called the 'pistol grip'.
The grip below is called the 'French grip'.

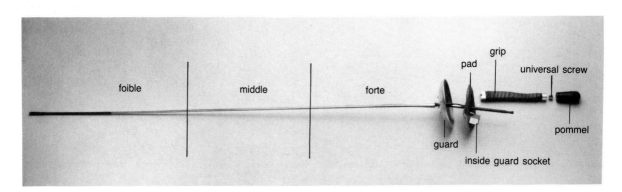

Fig 24   The various parts of a fencing weapon.

Fig 25 The inside and the outside target. Also marked is the nearest part of the target to attack.

most used of these are: on the sword-arm side, sixte (sixth), high line and octave (eighth), low line; and, on the non-sword-arm side, quarte (fourth), high line, and septime (seventh), low line. These terms are explained in greater detail later.

RIGHT OF WAY

The most difficult convention to understand is the right of way. The fencer making the original offensive action has the right of way if he starts extending the arm while continuously threatening the opponent's target. He loses the right of way if he bends his arm or ceases to threaten the target, or if the opponent beats or deflects the blade clear of the target. If two hits arrive at the same time, one of two things has happened: either the

Fig 26 British Ladies' Foil Championship, London 1985 – Linda Martin flèches at Kim Cecil.

fencers have attacked simultaneously or one fencer has attacked and the other has made an offensive action, a counter-attack.

If two fencers conceive and execute an attack simultaneously they have both committed a fault. The bout is stopped and no hit is awarded. They are placed back on guard and the bout is continued. When an attack is correctly executed with the arm straightening and point threatening the target, it has the right of way. If the opponent does not defend but attacks into it, the counter-attacker has committed a fault and this action will be given as 'out of time', irrespective of whether it has been made with a straight arm or whether it arrives before the attack. The bout is stopped, the fencer making the attack is awarded the hit, the contestants are placed back on guard and the bout is continued. (There *are* occasions when the counter attack will be given as 'in time' but this can only happen when an attack is made in two or more movements, and will be discussed later.)

To summarise, the foil is a conventional weapon, the conventions being the limited target and the right of way. It is a pointed weapon so it is carried as an extension of the arm. The object is to hit and not be hit. The conventions rule that the arm must be straightened when making an offensive action and hits may only be scored on a limited target. It is best to avoid the opponent's blade when attacking but to find it when defending.

5 How to Hold the Foil

The foil, being a balanced piece of sports equipment, is designed to fit into the sword hand so that it can be carried and not merely held. The old sword masters used to say: 'It is like a bird – if you hold it too tightly you will throttle it and if you don't hold it tightly enough it will fly away.' Look at the shape of the handle (the grip). It is curved to fit into the palm of the hand, allowing for the bulge of the thumb. Weapons are available for either right- or left-handed fencers.

Place the grip so that it rests on the second joint of the index finger with the shaping towards the thumb. Wrap the index finger around so that it touches three surfaces of the grip, then place your thumb along the top surface, the whole of the thumb lying flat. The thumb and the index finger are called the 'manipulators'. The other three fingers, the 'aids', rest on the side of the blade on the same plane as the tip of the index finger. The 'manipulators' move the point of the sword by a pushing and pulling movement while the 'aids' help to balance the weapon. The hand can be turned in a supinated (fingers uppermost) or pronated (back of the hand uppermost) position, or in any degree of these. The best position for executing bladework is to have the hand in the three-quarters-supination (henceforth called 'supination'). The thumb is turned

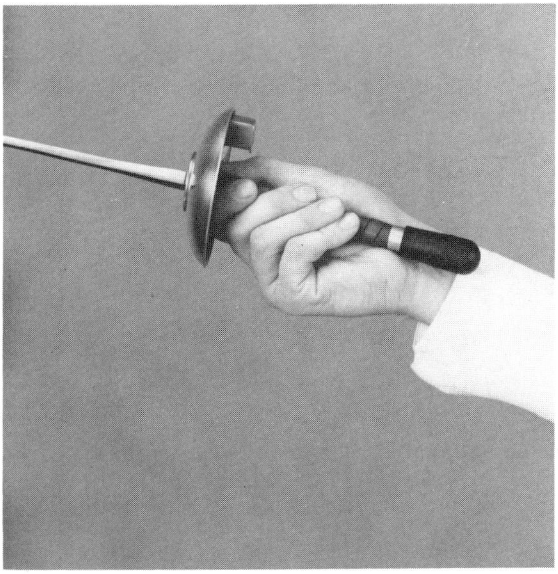

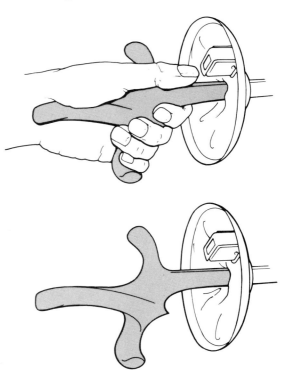

Fig 27   How to hold the foil – thumb on top, forefinger wrapped around, fingers laid along the side.

Fig 28   The pistol grip – the aids rest on the lower part of the grip.

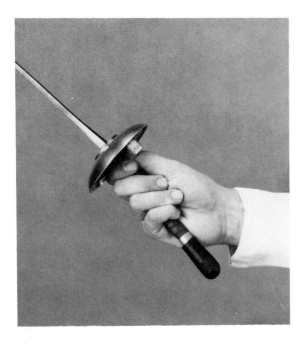

Fig 29 Shifting the grip before or whilst pronating in order to liberate the pommel from the wrist. This applies whether it is an orthopaedic or a French grip.

slightly to the side, with the corner of the blade uppermost.

For safety if a non-electric French grip foil or épée is used, in case the fencer is disarmed, the aids should pass through the small leather strap (martingale) attached to the foil.

The on guard position has been explained in Chapter 3. The position of the sword hand is breast-high and the sword is carried in a supinated position. The sword arm remains in line with the shoulder, leaving open only that part of the target which is on the inside of the blade. The outside of the blade (under the arm, the side and the back) is covered. As most attacks at foil are made on that strip of target just inside and just outside the blade, this position gives the best protection. The

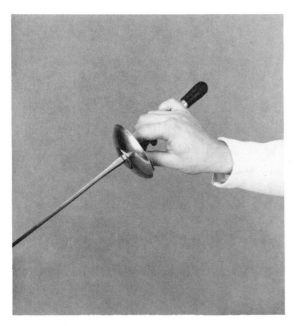

Fig 30 The pronated parry of seconde. Note the position of the pommel.

Fig 31 The eight positions at foil: 1–7, and low quarte, making 8. Quinte is added at sabre.

side on which the swords are either touching (engagement) or not touching (absence of blade) determines the line the fencers are in. There are eight lines, corresponding to the parry positions.

As a guide to the covered position, stand with the outside of the front foot and the heel of the back foot touching a wall. The sword arm should be held so that the outside of the guard is also touching the wall.

6 The Hit

The hit is the way the point of the foil strikes the target in order to score. You must hit clearly, with a pressure equivalent to 500 grams. This is best achieved by using the fingers. Holding the foil in the three-quarters-supinated position, push with the thumb while pulling with the forefinger. This has the effect of lowering the point (provided the aids are not gripping the handle so that it is unable to move). Move close to a convenient wall so that you can just hit the wall while the arm is bent. By moving the hand slightly forwards and pushing with the thumb and pulling with the forefinger, strike the wall cleanly with the point. Try to avoid straightening the arm more than is necessary to hit. A lot of practice will be needed to get a fast, clean and accurate hit on a selected target on the wall.

When you have completed this action successfully, gradually position yourself further away from the wall, straightening the arm in order to reach the target. At no time should the arm be so rigid that the elbow is locked. Every effort should be made to hit lightly, with as much bend in the blade as is necessary to score and no more; there should be no screwing action.

Now make the hit with a lunge. If possible, draw a life-size target on the wall and practise hitting the four quarters (lines) at will. Only when you can hit accurately and lightly should you start practising with another fencer, first at short distance, gradually extending until you are executing a full lunge. Your opponent can move backwards and forwards and on his signal (possibly dropping his sword arm), you hit, with or without a lunge according to the distance; even the length of the lunge may be varied.

The next progression is for both fencers to move, the attacker keeping distance and making his hit according to the signal. You have now accomplished the first of what are called the 'simple attacks' – the straight thrust.

Another method of hitting is to make what is called a 'flick hit'. To do this you need to use the wrist rather than the fingers, but it would be a mistake to take the fingers off altogether as you need them for balance and control. This method is particularly successful when making counter-attacks (described later), attacks or ripostes to the top of the shoulder or over the shoulder just on to the back. In fact, if your opponent ducks forwards whilst attempting to parry your attack, he will make his back vulnerable to the hit.

Start your practice, preferably against a lunging pad (a block of wood covered by a piece of soft material), by making a light stroking action with your wrist down the pad. Gradually change this stroking action into a striking action with the point, taking care to minimise the amount of point lift in order not to telegraph your intentions to your opponent. As you strike with the point, keep your hand above the height of the point; in fact, in some instances, you can make a see-sawing action with the point going down and the hand coming up. The ability to judge your reach is very important here: too close and you hit with the side of the blade, which does not register; too far away and you miss completely. A lot of practice is required – hitting at all distances, with a bent arm, a straight arm and a lunge. You should also practise the flick hit from all angles, your point flicking in sideways, upwards and downwards at various angles.

When making a parry and riposte, the parry can usually be used to position the point at the right angle to flick on to the target, making it unnecessary to lift the point beforehand.

When practising with a partner, make ripostes or attacks with or without a lunge, concentrating on hitting lightly at great speed to the top of the shoulder.

You can make this as an attack on your opponent's preparation. As your opponent steps forwards, make a flick hit by just straightening the arm without a lunge and, at the moment of point contact, move the back foot away very fast, jumping back or retiring rapidly. This action will be useful later when we deal with counter-attacks.

Flick hits can be done so lightly that the opponent often does not realise he has been hit and this should be your aim, for when they are executed clumsily they can hurt, and in any case are not successful.

7 Simple Attacks

Simple attacks consist of a single blade movement. There are four: the straight thrust, the only simple direct attack which goes straight to the target without deviation; the disengagement (commonly known as the disengage), which passes under the blade; the cut-over (coupé), which passes over the blade; and the counter-disengagement, which avoids the opponent's circular action. The last three of these are indirect attacks. With a little experimental work you will quickly realise that these are the only ways of hitting the opponent – straight through, under, over, or round.

It is important to remember that all attacks, especially those which are simple, should be made on a moving blade, but to facilitate the skills part of the action it is best to practise on a stationary blade at first.

THE STRAIGHT THRUST

This attack has been covered in Chapter 6.

THE DISENGAGEMENT

The object of this attack is to hit the opponent on the opposite side to that of the engagement by passing the blade under the opponent's. This is done by pushing with the thumb and pulling with the forefinger (which directs the point downwards) and pulling with the thumb and pushing with the forefinger (which raises it again), while straightening the arm to make the hit on target. You will have described a small V with the point while travelling under the opposing blade.

Starting at lunging distance (the distance you need to cover with the lunge in order to reach your opponent) with swords crossed, one of the fencers (the defender) adopts the covered position of sixte. The other (the attacker) passes his blade under his opponent's while straightening the arm and hits lightly and cleanly on the other side. Practise this until you can do it smoothly and fast, without leaning. The lunge should develop halfway through the straightening of the arm. Now practise hitting your opponent while he moves his blade slowly across the target.

As fencing is a combat sport, every action, no matter how technically made, will inevitably depend on timing, distance and the conditions created by the opponent. Always

The disengage

Fig 32   An outside engagement.

Fig 33 Whilst extending your arm, pass the blade under your opponent's, leading with the point.

Fig 34 Finish the lunge and hit in the new line.

practise in as competitive a situation as possible. Accordingly, once you have learned the basic movement of the disengagement, practise it on an opponent who is moving backwards and forwards, varying the time and distance of his movements. Remember: the disengagement takes up one period of fencing time so it has to be co-ordinated into one smooth movement.

Check List

- The hand must only just precede the foot.
- The blade should describe a helix. The ideal distance to do this is when the blades, if crossed, are foible to foible. If for some tactical reason you find yourself closer or further away than this, you will need to modify the lunge accordingly. Care must be taken to avoid developing a bent-arm attack at this stage of learning (*see* 'The Lunge' in Chapter 3).
- Balance must be maintained while lunging to avoid falling forwards.
- Shoulders should be kept in line to facilitate the point being accurately directed to any part of the target.
- Care should be taken not to exaggerate the lifting of the front hand higher than the shoulder.
- Avoid locking the elbow, which contracts the shoulder.
- Remember to carry the foil to the target without gripping it too tightly, maintaining a sensitive feel of the blade.
- Remember also the pressure from the point of an electric foil needed to make a hit is only 500 grams, so no screwing action is necessary.

THE CUT-OVER

This attack is made by passing the blade over your opponent's. Once again, start at lunging distance, with the blades engaged on the sixte side as before. Using the fingers and wrist, with a slight accompanying pull-back of the forearm, pass the blade over your opponent's, straightening the arm after the blade has passed over your opponent's point, and then direct the point with the fingers to make a clean hit. The height of the hand may vary and the hand may be rolled from supination to pronation or vice versa according to which part of your opponent's target you wish to hit – low line, high line, the left or right of the target, or the back. If, as a right-hander, you wish to hit another right-hander on the inside, whether high or low, it would be better to supinate the hand, whereas if you wish to hit under the arm or on the outside – the back – it is usually better to pronate the hand. In the case of a right-hander fencing a left-hander, or a left-hander versus a right-hander, the supination or pronation of the hand is reversed.

Once you have mastered the bladework, practise it with a step forward, with a lunge, and then with step forward and lunge. Then practise on a moving blade and a moving opponent.

Check List

- Ensure that you do not lunge until your arm begins to straighten.
- Using the wrist and fingers, let the point lead the hand so that it travels faster.
- The lunge needs continual checking to increase improvement and co-ordination with every attack.

THE COUNTER-DISENGAGEMENT

This particular action follows the circular movement of the opponent's blade, either deceiving the opponent's change of engagement or his circular parry to secure a hit.

At lunging distance, one fencer passes his blade under the opponent's in order to cover in the opposite line. As he does so, he moves

The counter-disengage

Fig 35 The cut-over – from the inside of the blade, pass your blade over the opponent's and hit on the outside.

Fig 36 The opponent changes the engagement from outside to inside, moving his hand to quarte.

Fig 37   Follow your opponent's blade around.

Fig 38   Hit in the original line which your opponent has inadvertently uncovered.

his arm and sword across to close the line completely. This defensive action is called a change of engagement. Practise two or three changes of engagement with your partner so that you get the feel of this movement.

The counter-disengagement is done as the opponent is changing the engagement. By following the defender's blade in the same direction, thus avoiding contact, you will be able to hit him in the line of the original engagement, which will now, of course, be open. The timing of this stroke is a critical factor for success. To get the timing right, you really have to anticipate when the opponent is going to move in order to deceive the blade. There are tactical ways of executing this stroke in order to time it

correctly, which will be discussed more fully later.

On your opponent's change of engagement, follow the blade round, using your fingers and extending your arm, co-ordinating the action with a smooth lunge to effect a hit.

Check List
- Ensure that the blade travels forwards as you circumnavigate the change of engagement.
- Use the fingers, minimising the amount of arm movement.
- Avoid contact with the opposing blade as the right of way might be lost.
- Check the lunge.

8 Defence

Defence can be effected in many ways: ducking under the opponent's attacking point, dodging sideways, stepping backwards, or blocking the way with your blade. The last of these is the parry.

There are four types of parry: the simple (instinctive) parry, the circular parry, the semicircular parry and the diagonal parry. With all of these parries, the principal part of the action is to oppose the foible of the opponent's attacking blade with the forte of one's own blade (*see* the illustration of parts of the foil on page 28). In this way, the opposing blade is controlled and dominated.

Fig 39 The parry of quarte. Note that the defence is effected by forte against foible.

The parries of sixte, quarte, octave and septime are executed with the hand in the three-quarters-supinated position. An equal number of parries are made with the hand in the pronated position. These are described in Chapter 16.

THE SIMPLE PARRY

This parry is made by the defender moving his blade from one side of the target to the other – from sixte to quarte or quarte to sixte (high line), or octave to septime or septime to octave (low line) – intercepting the opponent's blade forte against foible as it travels towards the target and deflecting it past the target.

Controlling the blade with the manipulators, move it across the body, keeping the point and hilt in line. In the high line the point must be above the hand and in the low line lower than the hand in order to control the attacking blade.

Allow the forearm to move with the blade, stopping just before it pulls the shoulder into movement. The point should finish just outside the opponent's target.

Check List
- Move the blade laterally with the point in line with the hilt.
- The hand should be breast-high in the high line, the blade forte to foible, to achieve maximum domination, and as near breast-high as possible in the low line for the same reason.
- In order to develop a sense of feel of the attacking blade, ensure that you do not grip the sword too tightly when parrying.

- Don't travel further than is necessary to deflect the attacking blade.
- To get maximum control, keep the arm bent while parrying.

THE CIRCULAR PARRY

As the name implies, the blade describes a complete circle. First of all, ensure that you are in a good covered position either in the sixte line or the quarte line. When your opponent attacks into the open line, use your fingers to make a complete circle with the blade by passing the point under the attacking blade and deflecting it, forte against foible. Manipulation of the blade should be done almost exclusively by the fingers, without movement of the arm or hand. If you make your parry like this and start in a correctly covered position, you will finish right and will deflect the blade successfully. If you move the arm or hand you may well not complete the parry, allowing the attacking point to come through and hit.

Practice is best with a partner; one makes an attack and the other practises the parry. In this way, the person attacking can be checking and re-checking his offensive action while the other is improving his defence.

The defender comes on guard covered in the sixte line, the attacker lunges with a straight thrust into the open line (aimed to hit but not too forcefully), and the defender blocks the attack with a circular parry. This is done by pushing and pulling with the thumb and forefinger and swinging the point in a circle while scooping up the attacking blade. The parry travels clockwise in sixte and anticlockwise in quarte. When you have practised it against the straight thrust, try using it against the disengage attack.

Check List
- Use the fingers as much as possible.
- Don't parry too soon or your opponent may deceive it.

The circular parry

Fig 40   The opponent attacks with a disengage.

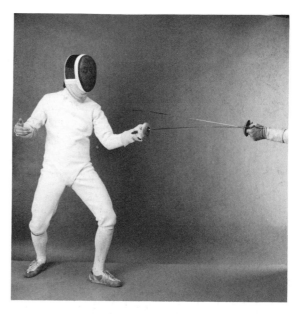

Fig 41   Pass your sword under your opponent's, making a complete circle.

Fig 42   Finish the circle to your original position, deflecting the attacking blade with the forte.

- Oppose the attacking foible with your own forte.
- Keep the hand breast-high.
- Don't allow the elbow to stick out.
- Finish in a good covered position.
- Don't step forwards at this stage.

THE SEMICIRCULAR PARRY

This parry describes a half-circle. The point of the sword can go from high to low line or from low to high line, depending on the guard position of your own blade. From sixte, the blade goes over your opponent's attacking point in the opposite direction to the circular parry. The difference is that the blade describes only half a circle – the point starts high and finishes low on the same side.

This parry is best done with the wrist and should be practised first without movement of the arm, the hand remaining breast-high.

Then, and then only, make a slight movement of the arm if necessary. If the attacking blade is coming in very low, perhaps angled upwards, it is sometimes necessary to drop the arm to supplement the movement of the wrist.

Practise this movement first in front of a mirror and then with a partner. Come on guard in sixte with the attacker covered in that line. He will make a disengage into the low line on which you will take your semicircular parry of octave. Change your guard position now to quarte, with attacker covered in that line, and when he attacks you with a disengage take the semicircular parry of septime.

Check List

- Keep the hand in three-quarters supination.
- Most of the movement is done with the wrist.
- Keep the hand breast-high.

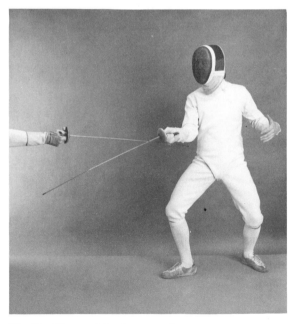

Fig 43   The semicircular parry from quarte to septime, taken over the top of attacking blade, deflecting it with the forte.

Fig 44 The semicircular parry from sixte to octave, taken over top of attacking blade, deflecting it with the forte.

- If you move the arm, take care to return to a covered position to ensure the clearance of the attacking blade.
- When travelling from high to low line, the point should finish well below the hand.
- When travelling from low to high line, the point should finish above the hand.
- Don't forget to use forte against foible.

PRONATED PARRIES

There is a set of parry positions used, at both foil and épée, that are made in pronation. They are prime, seconde and tierce, and may be taken as lateral, circular or semicircular parries. The principle of defence remains the same: you must parry with your own forte against the opponent's foible. These parries are particularly effective against someone who is forcing his blade with angulation through your defence, or at close quarters when it is not possible to keep your point in line with your forearm. When taking these parries, it is necessary to shift your grip so as to free the pommel from the wrist and get the correct angle of the blade in relation to the arm, as shown in the photograph. The shifting of the grip should be done whilst moving into pronation.

As these parries are of a very tactical nature, it is best to concentrate first on making good parries in three-quarter supination of sixte, quarte, octave and septime and gradually introduce the pronated parries as your proficiency grows and you mature as a fencer. In other words, don't run before you can walk.

The ripostes from pronated parries also need considerable experience – the distance is different, the angle of hitting is different, and usually to accomplish them well, requires very complicated body movements.

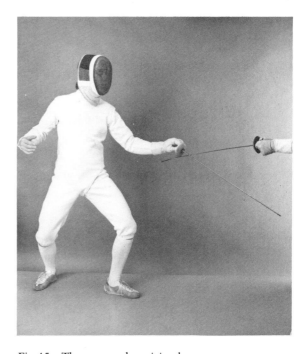

Fig 45 The pronated semicircular parry of seconde. This is an alternative to octave, especially when the attack is made with angulation.

43

Pronated Parries of Seconde

On your opponent's straight thrust into sixte, rotate your forearm, turning the hand inwards until the knuckles are uppermost. As you do so, deflect your opponent's blade with your forte. You will need to shift your grip as you rotate your forearm. Much practice will be needed to make this one smooth action; the hand must always remain at the same height.

Check List
- Rotate the hand from the forearm only.
- Shift the grip so as to liberate the pommel.
- Keep the height of the hand the same.
- Parry forte to foible.

THE DIAGONAL PARRY

The diagonal parry is usually taken from sixte to septime but can be executed from septime to sixte, from quarte to octave or from octave to quarte. The blade travels diagonally across the target, gathering the attacking blade into the forte on its way.

With a partner, come on guard in sixte. The attacker makes a disengage to the low line of quarte, on which the defender drops his point, travelling diagonally across the target to a position of septime and collecting the attacking blade on its way.

The defender now adopts the on guard position of octave. His opponent makes an attack into the high line of quarte, and the defender makes a diagonal parry of octave to quarte.

Check List
- This parry is executed mostly with the wrist, supplemented by the arm.
- The point action needs to be quite large but fluid, in order to scoop the attacking blade.
- The defender finishes in a good covered position, forte against foible.
- The hand should be kept in three-quarters supination.

ELEMENTARY TACTICS

It is important to understand which parry to use in a given situation and why. The majority of hits will be aimed at the strip of target just inside the arm. These attacks are best dealt with by using a circular or semicircular parry but they can also be parried by a simple parry of quarte. Attacks aimed at the area under the sword arm are best dealt with by the semicircular parry of octave. Attacks to the low inside area are best parried by a diagonal parry of septime. Nevertheless, any parry can be used to defend against a range of different attacks and the best tactical approach is to vary parries so that the opponent is unable to anticipate in which direction the blade will move.

The attacker, in his turn, must try to anticipate which way the defending blade will travel and frame his attack to deceive it. False attacks can be made to try to detect the opponent's pattern of defence – or an inspired guess can be made!

9 The Riposte

There are various ways by which an attacker can lose his right of way. One of them is when a defender beats or deflects the blade clear of the target. The parry does just this and gives the defender the right of way to launch the next offensive movement, the riposte, which is an offensive action after a parry.

Ripostes, like attacks, can be simple direct, indirect or compound.

THE DIRECT RIPOSTE

Having parried the blade, use the manipulators to direct the point to the target, following through with the hand and arm. The arm should be extended only as much as is required to reach the target with the point. In some cases it may be necessary to bend the arm even further if you are at close quarters. Remember that you have gained the right of way with the parry so obviating the necessity of straightening the arm.

The riposte may be done with or without a lunge, depending on the distance. One of the main causes of missing with the riposte is moving the front foot unnecessarily.

Practice

Get your opponent to make simple attacks, direct or indirect. Practise using the four types of parry you have learned and riposte direct. Remember that as it is a 'direct' riposte you need to develop speed in order to stop your opponent covering against your action. First practise riposting without a lunge, and then get your opponent to recover to guard after his attack, on which move-

ment you can practise lunging with your riposte.

Your opponent should now move backwards and forwards, with you trying to keep fencing distance. He will attack to hit and you will parry and riposte according to the distance. If you are very close, keep your arm bent; if further away, straighten it; and if he recovers to guard, lunge.

The attacker must always make an attack to hit; if he does not, you will certainly fail with your riposte. Sometimes, in practice, to ensure that this is happening, it is a good idea to try to catch your opponent out by not parrying as expected.

Check List
- It is essential to make a good parry as this is the foundation for a successful riposte.
- Control should be in the manipulators for good point direction.
- Fix an area of your opponent's target in your mind before riposting and try to hit just there.
- Don't move the front foot unless absolutely necessary.
- You do not need to straighten your arm to get the right of way; in fact, it may be necessary to bend it more before riposting.

INDIRECT RIPOSTES

Disengagement

The disengage riposte is executed against an attacker who, having been parried, returns to guard, covering against what he anticipates will be a direct riposte. It is timed to coincide with the withdrawal of the attacker's arm at the commencement of his simple parry.

Having parried the attack, feel the withdrawal of your opponent's blade and the start of his covering action and, using the manipulators, yield to the pressure of the closing line by disengaging under the blade, taking care not to straighten the arm at this stage. The manipulation of the blade is best done with the fingers, with a minimum of hand movement. If your parry is a semi-circular parry from high to low line, then your disengage riposte will be made over the blade and not under it. Having avoided your opponent's blade, straighten the arm as far as necessary in order to hit the opponent's target.

Practice

To learn the correct timing and feel of this movement, it is best to start the practice with your opponent staying on the lunge after delivering his attack and parrying your direct riposte. In this way you will feel his covering blade action and can change your direct riposte to a disengage riposte, successfully deceiving the parry.

As before, practise these ripostes with and without a lunge, then with movement.

Check List
- Make sure that your partner is attacking to hit.
- Use the manipulators to effect the disengage while making sure that you do not grip too tightly with the aids, as this will sky the point.
- The disengage may be made in the high or low line.
- Once again, don't move the front foot unless it is necessary.
- If at close quarters, it may be necessary to pull the forearm back to make the disengage.
- Don't straighten your arm until you have

successfully cleared your opponent's blade and arm.

The Cut-Over

The cut-over riposte is executed on the same opening as that of the disengage – on the attacker's attempt to take a simple parry – but in this case the blade passes over the opponent's point, whether in the high line or in the low line. As the opponent withdraws his arm to form a parry against the expected direct riposte, pass your blade over his by using the wrist. It may not be necessary to withdraw the forearm as when attacking with the cut-over because in this case your opponent's blade is moving away from yours, which enables you to clear it. As with the other ripostes, straighten your arm only enough to hit your opponent.

Practice

Start to practise without a lunge: your opponent stays on the lunge after his attack while you make your cut-over riposte on his covering movement. Vary your parries so that you can practise the riposte from a different line. Then introduce movement.

Check List
- The riposter must take control of the blade with the parry.
- Don't straighten the arm until you have cleared your opponent's blade and arm and point are in line with the target.
- Don't lift the point too high. It may be unnecessary to lift the point at all if the opponent's blade is moving away from you.
- Don't move the front foot unless it is necessary.
- As with the cut-over attack, the amount of supination or pronation of the hand will depend on the area you are aiming to hit. For instance, a cut-over under the sword arm or on the back will need to be

pronated whereas a riposte to the low line furthest from the sword arm should be supinated.

Counter-Disengage

The attacker who anticipates a direct riposte and instead of covering takes a circular (counter) parry will give the defender an opening for a counter-disengage riposte. To make this movement successfully, you must start your counter-disengage riposte fractionally after your opponent begins his circular parry, following his blade round until you are in line with the open target, whereupon you straighten your arm and hit.

Practice

For the correct timing of this riposte, which is essential, start as for the other indirect ripostes: the attacker stays on the lunge after making his attack and parries your direct riposte with a circular parry. Once you have a feel for your opponent's timing, deceive the circular parry with a counter-disengage riposte. Visualise the direction in which your blade must travel as this is a constant problem when first attempting this offensive action. Practice proceeds as with the other indirect ripostes: first riposte without a lunge and then introduce movement to get a more realistic action.

Check List
- Before making the riposte, visualise the direction in which your blade must travel.
- The parry is important to give you the feel of the blade.
- The riposte must be made with the fingers with a small blade action.
- Don't extend the arm until you have almost completely circumnavigated the attacker's blade and arm.

All ripostes may be executed with any form of footwork, including the flèche, depending on the circumstances. They may be performed with angulation, and they may be preceded by any of the preparations described in Chapter 13. Tactically, parries and ripostes are chosen as a means of hitting particular areas of the target which you have observed to be vulnerable.

All of the compound attacks described later can be done as compound ripostes, but, as with the indirect one blade movement ripostes, the arm must be kept bent whilst deceiving the opponent's blade, and must only straighten at the last moment as you hit, to avoid the opponent's arm.

FREE PLAY

Free play means using the strokes you have learned in a competitive situation.

1 To learn how to keep fencing distance you must have a partner. Tie a piece of string or tape so that it stretches slackly between you when you are both in the on guard position (without masks or foils). One leads, advancing and retiring, while the other keeps distance, not allowing the tape to become too taut or too slack. Take turns in leading.
2 To start developing your reactions and mobility make some wire or plastic hoops about 16 cm in diameter. One fencer holds the hoop behind his back while in the on guard position. The other fencer adopts the on guard position at lunging distance. The fencer with the hoop moves backwards and forwards, his partner keeping the distance. When the fencer holding the hoop raises it in front of him, his partner thrusts his hand through the hoop, using the necessary footwork to do so – without a lunge, with a lunge, with a flèche. At the beginning of the exercise the hoop should not be raised when it is impossible for the partner to respond but, as your footwork improves and speed increases and you develop quicker changes of direction, try to catch out your opponent by

raising the hoop so that he has to make fast adjustments in order to succeed. You can introduce a negative reaction by bringing a hand from behind your back without the hoop, in which case the opponent should do nothing. Each should take a turn at attacking.

3 The next stage of free play is performed with masks donned and with foils. The attacking fencer moves backwards and forwards, trying to induce the defender to make a mistake in keeping the distance. If, as the attacker, you can make your opponent close the distance and lose sense of it, you should have him at your mercy. Attack him with one of the actions you have learned, while he must defend himself with one of the defensive actions. In early practice it is best if one partner does all the attacking for a set period whilst the other defends. Change roles periodically.

Next, fence competitively until one partner makes five valid hits on the target of the other. You will need to agree between you whether the hits are 'good' – on target – or not; in free play it is customary to acknowledge good hits on oneself (it is the job of the president to award the hit in competitions). Remember that you must stop every time a hit is scored. If the hit lands off target it annuls any hit which follows.

As your free play tactics continue to develop, try to read your opponent's movements and make decisions as to the best way to outwit him. When you have decided on a plan, try to follow it to its logical conclusion. In this way you will learn about timing and tactics.

10 Compound Attacks

When describing simple attacks I said that you should attack an opponent while he is moving his blade and not while it is stationary. This is because the attacking blade must travel about a metre to reach the target while the defending blade has to travel only about 20 cm in order to parry and thus block the attack. Even though your opponent should not move his blade until the attack starts, there is little chance of hitting him before he parries unless time or distance can be gained, and various tactical ways of achieving this are discussed later. But if the opponent can be attacked whilst his blade is moving in an opposite direction to that of the attacking blade, the necessary time and distance are gained, provided the abilities of both fencers are roughly the same.

One way of doing this is to make one or more feints before the attack. (A feint attack is a blade movement made to resemble identically an attack in order to draw the defender to defend against it.) The definition of a compound attack is one that comprises one or more feints, ending with the hit. In fact it is a combination of simple attacks. Two disengages are called a one-two. A disengage followed by a counter-disengage is a doublé. Other compound attacks are named after their constituent parts – a feint of a direct attack followed by a disengage is a 'straight-thrust–disengage' (or a 'feint-direct–disengage'), and so on. Two, three, or even four feints may precede the attack, but multiple feints require footwork, and the more movements you make, the higher the risk of failure. For that reason only two-movement compound attacks (one feint followed by a movement that hits) are considered at this stage.

THE ONE-TWO

Probably the most common compound attack, the one-two consists of the feint of a disengage followed by a second disengage which deceives the opponent's simple parry. The deception of a parry is called a 'trompement'. If you have discovered that your simple disengage attacks are being met by simple parries, it is necessary to find a way of deceiving them in order to score a hit. Draw the parry with a feint of the disengage (the dummy attack), then, still using the fingers, deceive the lateral movement of the simple parry and hit in the opposite line. If the feint is going to draw your opponent into making the simple parry, it must look just like a disengage attack which will hit him unless he parries. The feint must be done with an extending arm and the disengage which forms the trompement must be done with the arm still extending, all of which must be completed during the lunge.

Practice

First practise the blade and arm action. Standing still, practise two disengages while straightening the arm. The arm should be straightening, but not necessarily straight. Do not lock the elbow and/or the shoulder. Keep practising this until you have a smooth, fast, continuous action. Do not lean, twist or move the body. Once you have achieved this, you must introduce the lunge. Now you need an opponent to practise with. The sword hand should start travelling forward slightly before the foot starts moving, and the feint must be held while travelling forward until the opponent's parry starts. Use only the fingers to manipulate the point and try to hit the target before the front foot lands and stops moving. Practise hitting in both high and low lines. The complete action should take one period of fencing time, the time it takes to perform one movement. If you lunge with an attack, remember that the lunge takes one period of fencing time. Whatever you do with your blade from the start to the finish of the lunge will be done in that one period of fencing time.

Check List
- Use the fingers to manipulate the blade with a minimum of hand and arm movement, describing small Vs with the point.
- The arm must be straightening to secure the right of way.
- Minimise the amount of upper body movement.
- The lunge should accelerate to the conclusion of the attack.
- A swinging shoulder will destroy your accuracy.

THE DOUBLÉ

This attack, also called the disengage–counter-disengage, is executed against an opponent who takes circular parries. The method is similar to the one-two in that a feint of the disengage is made to draw the parry, followed by a counter-disengage to deceive the circular movement. The blade actions are made with the fingers as before, with the accent on a controlled, progressive attack. Again, a feint disengage must have the appearance of a simple attack meant to hit. The attack must be accomplished with the minimum of drift with the point, so ensuring a smooth and effective offensive movement.

Practice

Practise this in the same way as you did with the one-two, concentrating on making a good feint to draw your opponent's response. If you manipulate the point with your fingers so that it continuously threatens the valid target, concentrating on making the attack progressive and in one period of fencing time, you will achieve a good compound attack.

Check List
- Use the fingers to manipulate the blade.
- Hold on to the feint for as long as possible, keeping the blade threatening the target.
- Remember that the straightening arm secures the right of way.
- Try not to lean.
- Take care not to let the point get caught up on your opponent's arm when executing the counter-disengage and don't bend your arm.
- Check the lunge constantly to develop an effective attack.

11 Successive Parries

Parries, identical or different, which follow each other in succession constitute the defence against the compound attack. The defender parries the feint or feints and the final line of attack. If you know that your opponent is going to make a compound attack you have several options open to you, one of which is to parry. If you perceive what compound attack your opponent is about to make, you have the choice of the final line into which you take the attacking blade. There could be various tactical reasons why you wish to finish in a particular line so you choose your parries accordingly. It is always best to make successive parries compatible with the attack. If it is known that a fencer is going to make a one-two attack, the first parry should be a lateral parry. If, on the other hand, he is making a doublé attack, your first parry should be a circular parry. If such a pattern is not followed, there is an inevitable clash of blades in which either attacker or defender might be hit. To gain the time to complete the successive parries, it is usually best to step back with them.

Practice

Start by getting your partner to make one-two attacks on which you take two simple parries in succession, finishing in a good covered position. Keep the blade movements small and under control, remembering to parry forte against the attacking foible. When you have accomplished this successfully, change the second parry to a circular parry and, finally, to a semicircular parry. You will note that by altering the final parry you can take your opponent's blade into another line. This will be discussed more fully under 'Tactics' in Chapter 13. Once you have successfully completed two parries, get your partner to extend his compound attack with an extra blade movement – for example a one-two-three – against which you can try taking three parries in succession. You should then add ripostes to follow your parries. A step back with the first parry will give you more time to riposte.

Check List
- Parry forte to foible.
- Ensure the feel of the blade through the manipulators.
- Keep the hand well forward when taking the parries.
- Concentrate on timing to ensure complete domination of the blade.
- Refer to Chapter 8 on parries.
- Step back smoothly to a distance from which you can riposte easily. The rear foot should move as you start the first parry.

12 Counter-Ripostes

The counter-riposte is the offensive action following a successful parry of the riposte. Only one riposte is made after a successful parry of the attack. All other offensive actions made after parries are counter-ripostes, and they are numbered. Since the first is made by the original attacker, all even-numbered ripostes come from the defender. This is the start of what is known as a fencing 'phrase', a series of blade movements which may or may not result in a hit, similar to a rally in tennis. Like ripostes, counter-ripostes can be direct, indirect or compound.

The counter-riposte

Fig 46   The attack is first parried.

Practice

The First Counter-Riposte Direct

Make a disengage attack and stay on the lunge, keeping your body upright and well balanced. Your partner should take a simple parry and riposte direct, against which you also take a simple parry and riposte direct to hit.

The Second Counter-Riposte Direct

This time your partner attacks and stays on the lunge, receives your riposte with a simple

Fig 47   The riposte is then parried.

Fig 48   The offensive reply is the counter-riposte.

parry and ripostes. You parry this riposte and hit with the second counter-riposte.

Now practise the counter-riposte by disengage and cut-over on your opponent's simple parry, then by deceiving his circular parry with a counter-riposte by counter-disengagement.

Check List
- See Chapter 8 on parries and Chapter 9 on ripostes.

13 Preparations

Every stroke, offensive or defensive, must be the right stroke executed at the right distance and time. Distance and time are linked: time affects distance and distance affects time. If a stroke is technically weak but is the right stroke executed at the right time and distance, it may well succeed. The same cannot be said of the reverse. Preparations are a method of gaining time and distance. They comprise making and breaking ground (footwork), attacks on the blade (beat and pressure), and takings of the blade (bind, envelopment and croisé). The preparations themselves do not hit the opponent but open the way for a hit to be made.

MAKING AND BREAKING GROUND

One way of making or breaking ground is to use the techniques of stepping forwards and backwards, and jumping forwards and backwards described in Chapter 3. A variation is to use a much lighter, dancing type of footwork, which enables you to make slight variations in distance to get to the right distance at the right time. By making your footwork more of a dancing action performed on the balls of the feet you can adjust the distance your feet move in relation to each other, the rhythm of the footwork, and your distance from your opponent. This type of footwork makes it much easier to change to a jump or flèche before your opponent belatedly realises what you are doing.

ATTACKS ON THE BLADE

These preparations are ideal for drawing a reaction from the opponent's blade. There are two, the beat and the pressure. When you attack the blade, your opponent will either be taken by surprise and leave an opening for a direct thrust or he will oppose the preparation, thus inviting an indirect attack.

The Beat

The beat is striking the opponent's blade, foible to foible. The strike should be made cleanly by detachment. The easiest way to do this is to rotate the wrist just enough to be able to strike. Do not move the arm more than necessary and keep control of the point.

If your opponent does not react, the way is open to make a direct thrust. If he returns the beat your attack will be made by disengagement or cut-over, and if he changes the engagement the attack will be by counter-disengagement.

Practice

Starting at close quarters, practise beating your opponent's blade, concentrating upon making it a surprise action in a crisp, explosive manner. No undue force should be used with this movement and the point should be kept strictly under control, so the sword arm must not travel across the body. The beating action will strike slightly on top of the blade to give more dominance.

Now follow the beat with a straight thrust, disengagement, cut-over, or counter-disengagement depending on your opponent's reaction.

Now add footwork, such as steps forwards or ballestras, making the beat while moving forwards but before the lunge. You can try changing the engagement before making the beat.

Check List
- Ensure that the beat is made against your opponent's foible.
- Try not to move the arm more than is necessary.
- Do not follow through with your blade, but allow it to detach from your opponent's blade.
- Keep the point under control ready for the attack.

The Pressure

As most fencers fence with absence of blade, they are usually too far apart to make blade contact. Therefore it may be necessary to engage the blade first (*see* 'Takings of the Blade' on page 57). The pressure is best executed against your opponent's foible, with a subtle pushing action, taking him by surprise and forcing him to make an instinctive response. Once again, this action is achieved by a slight rotation of the wrist.

Practice

The pressure is similar to the beat except that it is made in engagement, while the beat – as its name implies – is a striking action.

The Froissement

The froissement is similar to the beat but the strike is made at much more of an angle and slides down the opposing blade forcefully. It is best done as a form of simple attack or counter-attack when a response is not required from the opponent. The effect is to brush the opposing blade aside.

The froissement is best executed on the outside line. For greater power it is best to supinate as you strike and slide down the blade to the target.

Practice

Work with a partner at riposting distance, your opponent covered in sixte. Disengage or cut-over the opposing blade, then strike it against the foible with the middle of your own blade. The action, a combination of a beat and a graze (*see* below) should be oblique and forceful. It ends with your forte sliding down the opposing blade in the final action of the deflection. This is not at all a subtle movement and may, if badly timed, disarm your opponent before you have the opportunity to hit him.

Practise this action at riposting distance until it is clean and swift. Rotate the wrist and supinate the hand to increase the power of the froissement. Gradually introduce a lunge, and then execute the action with a lunge on your opponent's step forward as a form of 'attack on the preparation'.

Check List
- Judge your distance very carefully: it is the same as for a simple attack.
- Strike the opponent's blade in the right place, preferably on the foible with at least the middle of your blade or the forte.
- Rotate your wrist to increase the power.
- Take care not to disarm your opponent.

The Coulé

The coulé may be classified as an attack on the blade or a taking of the blade (prise de fer) and, like the pressure, to which it is very similar, it is quite a subtle movement. The English name for the coulé is 'the graze', which describes the method of making this attack. You graze your blade right down from the tip to the base of the opposing blade, pushing it aside as you do so. This attack may be followed by a straight thrust;

it is also a very effective feint of the straight-thrust–disengage, as the sideways movement of the opponent's blade usually results in his returning the pressure, opening the way for an indirect or compound attack.

Practice

It is usually more effective to make this attack on a closed line so it is best done on the outside line – the only line closed in modern foil fencing.

As with the pressure, you must either engage the blade first, or make some blade action such as a disengage or cut-over, to position your blade on the outside of the opponent's. Having done this, slide your blade down the opposing blade, engaging your middle or forte against his foible. As you get near to his target, you will have dominated his blade with your own.

Start at riposting distance, stepping forwards with the graze. When this is going smoothly, lunge.

Then practise making a graze–disengage. For this, your opponent must oppose your graze and when you change to a one-two he must oppose and parry.

Check List
- In order to make this stroke effective, you must engage the blade in such a way that you disguise your true intention.
- Engage the middle or forte of your own blade against your opponent's foible.
- The graze – whether direct, indirect or compound – must be executed as one smooth act going forwards.
- If necessary, use your wrist.

The Dérobement

The dérobement is an evasion of your opponent's attempt to take your blade and is usually done when your blade is in line. Being in line means that your arm is straight and your point threatening your opponent's target. In this position you have 'priority of the line', so, in order to attack you, your opponent must first move your point out of line either with a beat or a taking of the blade (a prise de fer). You retain the priority if you can evade this beat or taking of the blade by means of a dérobement.

Dérobements look very simple actions but you will find them nearly impossible to execute unless you know exactly which way your opponent is going to take or beat your blade. The stroke requires very fast reactions and good perception. Some fencers are extremely adept at dérobements while others find them very difficult to execute.

Practice

Straighten your arm, sword in line, point threatening the opponent's target. Invite your opponent or partner to step forwards and engage your blade. Deceive this movement by manipulating your blade, preferably with the fingers, since to retain the right of way you must ensure that you threaten the target at all times. You lose the right of way if, when you deceive your opponent's blade, your movement is so wide that your point is aimed away from the target.

Once you are used to deceiving the blade one way, ask your opponent to change his action so that you may practise deceiving it in another way. Then get your opponent to make a series of attempts to take your blade and see if you can succeed with compound blade actions.

The only way to improve your execution of dérobements is continual practice to improve your perception and reactions.

Check List
- Make sure that your point threatens the target throughout the whole movement.
- Do not bend your arm, as this will lose you the right of way. This is a common fault.
- To ensure that your point doesn't wander

off target, make the dérobement with the fingers and the minimum of wrist.

- Beware that your opponent doesn't duck or twist as you make your hit.
- It is a fallacy to think that stepping back while executing a dérobement loses you the right of way.

TAKINGS OF THE BLADE
(Prises de Fer)

A poorly executed attack on the blade brings the risk of losing control of your opponent's blade and walking on to his point. A safer preparation is to take the blade rather than attack it. There are four basic ways of taking the blade: the engagement, the envelopment, the bind, and the croisé.

The Engagement

Blades are said to be engaged when they are in contact. When an engagement is used as a preparation of attack, the blade may be taken in any guard position, covered or uncovered (*see* Chapter 5).

As with the beat, no more arm movement than is tactically required should be used when executing an engagement as a preparation for an offensive action. As the engagement is a prelude to an attack, it needs to be taken in an offensive manner, rather than in a defensive manner.

An engagement executed on stepping forwards may serve two purposes: to hold your opponent's attention, thus masking your true intention, and as a safety precaution to avoid walking on to his blade.

Practice

Step forwards and engage your opponent's blade in quarte by taking it foible to foible, but do not move your hand and arm across to the quarte position. Your blade will be diagonally across the target.

Fig 49   The engagement – when the blades are in contact with one another.

Now step forwards, changing the engagement to sixte.

When you can do this neatly, controlling the opponent's blade, try an engagement, a change of engagement and variations of these movements, all the time feeling your opponent's blade through your fingers (sentiment de fer), recognising any reactions that he may make involuntarily. Then exploit those reactions with direct, indirect, and compound attacks.

Check List
- Engage foible to foible.
- Avoid moving the arm across the target.
- Develop the feel of the blade, seeking out your opponent's reactions.
- Take the blade swiftly and without prior warning to avoid the possibility of your opponent deceiving your preparation.

The defence against takings of the blade is explained in detail in Chapter 21.

The Bind

The bind is probably the easiest of the takings of the blade. The action takes the opposing blade across the body from the high to the low line or from the low to the high line. It is best executed on an opponent who has a straight arm, blade in line. Taking the blade requires a certain amount of resistance so it is used against continuations or renewals of attack as well as against blades that are held in line, threatening the target.

Since taking the blade gives you complete control of your opponent's weapon it is usually safer than attacking his blade with a beat or pressure.

On your opponent's straight arm (his point threatening your target), engage the blade in quarte forte to foible, using the wrist. Rotate your blade over the top of your

Fig 51 Rotate your blade over the top of your opponent's.

The riposte by bind

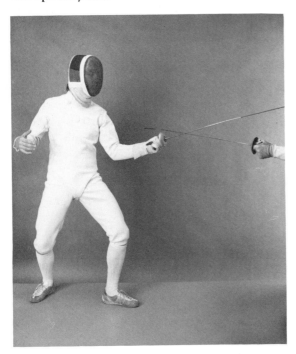

Fig 50 The parry of sixte.

Fig 52 The riposte is made into septime, sliding down the opponent's blade.

opponent's and diagonally across the body to the position of octave, maintaining contact with the blade and with your hand in supination. (It is also possible to make this preparation from octave to quarte, but it would be dangerous from sixte to septime or from septime to sixte, right-hander to right-hander.) You can now execute a straight thrust or an indirect or compound attack.

Two left-handers will make the takings of the blade in the same lines as above but a right-hander against a left-hander would find it better to make the prise de fer from sixte to septime and from septime to sixte because of the angle of the blade. Vice versa for a left-hander against a right-hander.

Practice

It is best to start learning this action at close quarters with a fencer holding his arm straight, point threatening the target. First of all, you can take the blade as above and step forwards with the hit. Then change to a short lunge. Next step forwards and engage the blade, bind and lunge.

The bind is also very useful as a preparation for a riposte. When your opponent attacks you, parry, bind and hit with the riposte. This is especially useful as an answer to a remise.

Check List
- Ensure that your opponent's foible is well locked into your forte.
- To keep the foible in the forte, use your wrist, not your fingers, making the point describe as large a circular action as possible.
- It may be necessary to straighten the front leg slightly so that your opponent's blade can be cleared past it.
- The bind is best taken against a straight arm which is unlikely to bend.
- Whether you hit under or over the arm will depend on the height of the opponent's blade when you take it.

- It is vitally important to maintain contact with the opposing blade, thus dominating it.

The Croisé

In the croisé the blade is taken from the high to the low line or from the low to the high line on the same side. It is a very useful action at close quarters, especially when the bout is between a right- and a left-hander. It is also very effective with angulation. Make sure that the foible of your opponent's blade is taken by your forte and that contact and dominance of the blade is maintained throughout. A croisé from high to low line can be made on someone whose arm is very high.

Practice

Start as with the bind, with your opponent at close quarters and with his arm straight. Take his blade in quarte, again using your wrist, pivot over the top and push it down with the forte of your own blade. You may need to lower your body by bending your knees deeper to increase the dominance.

Next practise parrying your opponent's blade in quarte and riposting with a croisé.

It is also very effective to parry quarte on the lunge and riposte with a croisé.

Check List
- As with the bind, choose this action only against someone with a straight arm, point threatening the target continuously.
- Maintain contact throughout.
- Dominate your opponent's blade by applying forte to foible.

The Envelopment

The envelopment requires a very definite blade presentation on the part of the attacker, whose hand must be slightly low, exposing just a little target above it. This preparation

Fig 53   A prise de fer attack with a flèche – Commonwealth
Fencing Championships.

finishes in the same line as the blade is taken – sixte to sixte or, rarely, octave to octave. Engage your opponent's blade in sixte, make a complete circle, using the wrist, ensuring that you maintain contact as you pass your own blade over the opponent's arm and hit in the sixte line.

Practice

As with the other takings of the blade, start with your opponent at close quarters, sword in line, his arm straight and lower than before. Take his blade in sixte with the forte of your own, encircle it completely using your wrist and maintaining contact and dominance, then straighten your arm and hit in the high line of sixte. Once you have successfully practised this, as with the other actions, first lunge with the taking of the blade. Then parry sixte and riposte by envelopment.

Check List
- Take the opponent's blade forte to foible.
- Make the envelopment using the wrist, describing as big a circle as possible with the point.
- Be careful to keep contact with the opposing blade as you slide through to hit in sixte.

COUNTER-ATTACKS

Counter-attacks are offensive actions made into offensive actions. An attack into an attack is called a stop hit; an offensive action into a riposte or a renewal of attack is simply called a counter-attack.

Stop Hits

An attack that is an initial offensive action made by extending the arm and continuously threatening the target has the right of way unless it is parried or beaten out of line. If the attacking blade is not beaten or parried, but the defender attacks into it with the result that both fencers are hit, the defender's action constitutes a stop hit and is a valid hit only if it is in time – that is, it must arrive a period of fencing time before the final movement of the initial attack. If this timing is not correct the stop hit is out of time and is disregarded, in which case the initial attacker's hit is valid. As it is extremely difficult to make a stop hit in time, it is safer to avoid the attacking blade by ducking or twisting as you make the stop hit or to hit and jump back or move away so fast that the opponent's ·blade does not arrive.

Practice

On your opponent's attack duck right down low at the very last moment and stop hit in the low line. Having successfully avoided the blade by ducking, practise the same action but by twisting. Both the duck and the twist must be done at the very last moment or your opponent's blade will follow you. The next action is to hit the opponent and jump back out of distance immediately so that the opposing blade falls well short of your target.

Check List
- The success of all counter-attacks depends on complete surprise. They should be so well in time or catch the opponent in such a way that they completely arrest the attack.
- Speed of hitting is essential so you must practise this – it is the key to all good fencing.
- Sense of distance is vitally important as you must assess whether your opponent can reach you or not.

Stop Hits in Opposition

These can be executed in exactly the same way as the stop hits. The difference is that you must first anticipate the final line of your opponent's attack and close out this line as you hit with the counter-attack.

Practice

Instead of twisting or ducking as you make your counter-attack on a straight thrust, attack with a disengage right at the beginning of the attack. Don't allow your arm to swing across your body but keep it in line with your shoulder. Provided your opponent's hand is slightly lower than his shoulder, you will intercept his foible with your forte and your blade will slide through to the target, deflecting the attacking blade. The same action can be performed against an opponent who is executing an attack by disengagement or cut-over. The difference here is he is going under or over your blade so all you need to do to block out the opposing blade is to make a direct attack, sword in line, and once again you will deflect it with your forte.

In some instances it may be necessary to lunge, close the distance or step forward with this form of counter-attack, so practise making it at all distances.

Check List
- Timing again is essential to ensure that you meet your opponent's foible with your own forte. Take care not to do the reverse as you will not deflect his point but will move on to it.
- Sense of distance is very important as not only must you assess your own ability to reach his target but you must do so having taken his foible with your forte.

DEFENCE AGAINST COUNTER-ATTACKS

If the counter-attack is a stop hit, the easiest defence is to prevent its being made in time. If you anticipate a stop hit, and make a simple attack instead of the compound attack which your opponent is expecting or, if you see the stop hit coming whilst making your attack, finish the attack immediately, thus preventing the stop hit arriving one period of fencing time before the final movement.

It is also possible to deal with counter-attacks by anticipating them and parrying and riposting.

Pronated Parries

Pronated parries are dealt with in detail in Chapter 8.

OBSERVATIONS ON FOIL TACTICS

Tactics in fencing, as in combat sports, consist of bluffing your opponent into giving you the openings you require in order to score hits. They can be used to draw the opponent towards you, to keep him at distance, or to draw him on to your attack or on to your riposte. Your object is to dominate the play and impose your will on the bout.

It is best to practise tactical fencing every time you fight a bout. Try to analyse your opponent's movements, how he responds to your attacks, what attacks he makes, his distance and timing. Seek out his bad habits, especially those he cannot control. While doing this, keep your distance and vary your defence. Don't forget that your opponent is probably doing the same thing.

Start by observing fencers, not only while you are fencing with them but while they are fencing with others. You must be very observant and recognise exactly what they do – not only their bladework but their footwork too. Note whether they lean, the height of their hand and the angle and timing of the hits they make. Test yourself to see how accurate your observations are, either by noting them down in a notebook or –

Fig 54   Rossi of Italy shouts in triumph as he beats his compatriot, Scuri.

even better – by recording them with a video camera.

See how quickly you can find an answer to your opponent's actions. You can sometimes discuss tactics with more experienced fencers or fencing coaches, recounting your observations and seeing whether they agree – not only with what you have seen but also with your conclusions.

When you have the opportunity to fence with a fencer you have already observed, put your own tactics to the test and see for yourself whether you have analysed the play correctly. At first you will probably find only minimum success, but persevere. If an action you have chosen fails it is not necessarily because it is the wrong stroke; it may be the correct stroke executed with wrong timing, distance, or both – or simply badly executed.

Increasing experience will tell you which part of an action you need to change, or whether to reject it completely. It is essential to be able to speed up your decision making, especially when you are losing a bout and under pressure.

The following exercise will improve your memory and speed up your decision making.

Working with a partner, when one fencer makes an attack, the other parries and makes a riposte as near as possible to the original attacking stroke – if it is a direct attack, the riposte should be simple and direct; if the attack is made by a disengagement, the riposte should be made by disengagement. The original attacker counter-ripostes with the same action and the defender does likewise. When the attacker is ready, he changes his counter-riposte and the defender has to change his action immediately to match it. Introduce as many different strokes and forms of footwork as you can. Each time there is a change, the opponent must recognise the change and repeat it exactly.

If you perceive a weakness in an opponent's defence, it may be an advantage to change the line of engagement in order to attack directly or indirectly into that weak area. This can be brought about either by changing the engagement masked by other preparations (such as stepping forwards, stepping backwards, and so on), or by selecting the right parry, whether a single parry or the last parry, or a succession of parries.

PART THREE
THE ÉPÉE

14 Characteristics of Épée Fencing

Like the foil, the épée is a pointed weapon. It has a much larger guard than the foil and the blade does not come out of the centre of the guard as it does with the foil but is mounted eccentrically. The blade itself is fluted and roughly triangular in section, unlike the blade of the foil, which is square.

Using the épée is similar to using the foil and I shall consider in detail only the differences in technique, and in describing each stroke I shall draw parallels with the foil skills. Today all competitive épée fencing is done with electric weapons since spotting hits by eye alone is very difficult.

The chief characteristic of the épée is that it is bound by none of the conventions which govern the foil and the sabre. The épée was always a duelling weapon; there is no right of way and, since any hit would cause a wound, double hits are valid. With modern electric épées scores are recorded by an electric apparatus and a timer distinguishes between double and single hits. If two hits are made simultaneously a double hit is scored but if the delay between the two hits is more than $\frac{1}{25}$ second only the first hit is valid.

The whole body is the target; you can hit your opponent on the toe or on the hand or even on the head. Hits are made only with the point of the sword, just as at foil. Most competitions are fenced on a metal strip which shorts out when struck by the point of the sword, registering no hit. When an épéeist makes a very fast attack at foot only the electric recorder can register whether the point hits the foot or the floor.

There are occasions when an épéeist wishes to score a double hit for tactical reasons. If a fencer leads 4–0 and a double

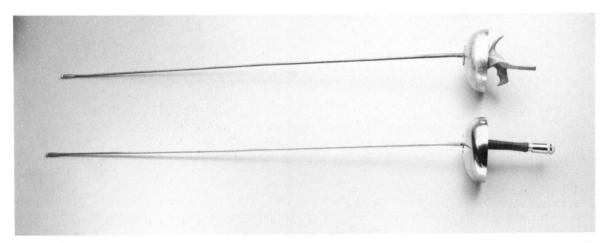

Fig 55 Épées with pistol grip and French grip.

Fig 56   De Bunsen (right) of England just outreaches Philion of
Canada in the final of the ladies' épée at the Commonwealth
Championships, 1986.

hit would give him victory at 5–1, in the
early rounds of a competition he may choose
to save energy in this way. However, at all
three weapons in fencing we try to hit and
not be hit, which, after all, is the basis of
good swordplay. Certainly at épée if your
opponent is ahead on points you must hit
and not be hit.

If both fencers need only one hit for
victory (for example, if they are 4 all in a 5-
point bout) and both then score with a
double hit, the score becomes 5 all and they
go back on guard to fence for one more hit.
At this stage double hits are disregarded for
scoring and the fencers resume the bout until
a single hit gives one of them victory. In such
a bout the final score is given as 5 V (victory)
against 5 D (defeat).

All fencing bouts are fought within a time
limit, depending on how many hits are being
fought for. If when time is called both
épéeists are equal on points, both lose the
fight. This is called a double defeat and the
score is written as 5 D (defeat) against each
fencer. If the time limit is near one épéeist
must get a single hit before time is called in
order to win; a double might well lose the
fight for both contestants.

The character of épée fencing is defined
above all by these three factors: the whole
body is the target; double hits are valid; and
double defeats are possible. The épéeist must
learn from the outset that one of the safest
ways of hitting without being hit is to take
the opponent's blade and hit whilst holding
it off one's own target. He must learn to be

67

accurate enough to hit at will the extremities of the target such as the hand, the toe or the knee. And he must realise that attacking the trunk of the body carries the risk of the opponent scoring a single hit on his hand before his own hit registers. The converse also holds good and a fencer leading on hits can win the fight with a hit to the opponent's hand when he is coming for the body, even at the risk of a double hit. However, it would be even better to take the blade and hit the opponent in opposition on the wrist so that his attack cannot arrive.

HOW TO HOLD THE ÉPÉE

The épée is held in exactly the same way as the foil: the index finger is wrapped round the grip, the thumb is placed flat on top (these are the manipulators) and the remaining three fingers (the aids) lie on the side of the grip. Although the thumb rests near to the pad, there are occasions when an épéeist finds it expedient to gain extra reach by holding the épée further back on the handle, which can be achieved only after much practice.

THE ON GUARD POSITION

The position of the arms, feet, trunk and head is common to all three weapons and is described in Chapter 3. The only difference with the épée is that the hand may be carried a little further forward than with the foil. I do not favour keeping the sword arm completely straight. With hand slightly forward a more effective clearing of the toe can be achieved when taking low line parries.

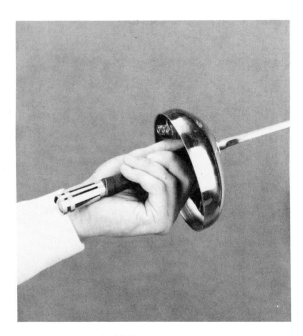

Fig 57   How to hold the épée. As you can see, the épée grip is similar to that of foil. This applies to the pistol grip also.

Fig 58   The on guard position is the same for the épée as for the foil, except that the sword hand may be held slightly further forward.

THE HIT

The hit with the épée is almost the same as with the foil but in some instances, a little more wrist may be used in order to achieve the angulation to hit over the top of the guard or round the side of the guard to hit the hand. It is also possible to use the wrist to flick the blade to various areas, especially those of the forward target. (For a more detailed description of these 'flick hits' *see* Chapter 6.)

The skill of hitting a horizontal target such as the top of the arm takes a long time to develop, so the sooner you start practising it the better. For the occasions when you have no partner to practise with, make up a padded area to represent the top of an arm. Start by hitting a vertical surface and gradually move down to the horizontal. At first you will find that you have to lift the hand to get the blade at the right angle to hit the horizontal. Use the fingers as described for the foil and supplement this with a little bit of wrist. As you practise, try to lower the hand each time until you are hitting the horizontal surface with as low a hand as possible so as not to uncover the lower part of your arm.

Refer to the foil section constantly and use the practices described in Chapter 6.

15 Offensive Actions

At épée the target is split into three main areas, corresponding roughly with the depth to which the attack will have to travel. The first area, the forward target area, comprises the front foot, leg, arm and hand. The next area is the main trunk – plus the head. The third area of the target is the rear leg and arm and the back. To hit these areas, the same types of offensive action as with the foil are used, though of course the length of the lunge and where you make the hit differ. For example, you could make a disengagement to the hand, to the front arm, to the body, or underneath the front arm, or you could direct it to the rear arm or rear leg. The last two options are unusual unless you get to very close quarters or, for some tactical reason, you find this the best area to hit. However, in recent years the distance at épée has tended to become a little closer and there have been far more attacks to the body than there were previously. This probably results from the growing athleticism of fencers, who nowadays are much faster in delivering attacks and are much less at risk when going to the body.

THE STRAIGHT THRUST

The straight thrust is described at the beginning of Chapter 6. The attack at épée is very much the same, though of course it is much more difficult to hit someone to the hand or even to the forearm than to the body. If your opponent is on guard correctly and therefore covering his hand with his guard, that guard will probably cover a lot of his forearm as well, so in order to hit him with a straight thrust on the hand you have to angulate your point slightly round his guard. This is a little risky since while you are angulating round to hit him you are exposing your own arm to a straight thrust from your opponent. His answer might well be a stop hit in opposition, which closes that line and hits you at the same time.

Practise the straight thrust attacks to the arm in order to get the necessary speed. Attack on to the top of the arm, to the outside of the arm, to the inside of the arm, and underneath the arm. Some of these attacks are very similar to a disengagement, and in many cases they take the form of a disengagement.

There are two basic methods of executing the straight thrust. The first is to allow your point to travel before your hand (as with the foil) and then to raise your hand very slightly as you go for the hit so that your point dips down over the top of the guard to hit your opponent on the top of his arm; alternatively, start with the point and then allow your hand to move slightly to the side so as to angulate round the guard on the inside. The second method is to make a flick hit. Flick hitting is very useful at épée but must not be overdone – if you use this type of hit all the time your opponent will soon get wise to your strategy. Indeed, this is so with any move in fencing: if you use a particular stroke constantly the opponent will very quickly find an answer to it. The occasional flick hit is however a very useful tactic.

Flick hits require a lot of practice. You must flick the point partly with the fingers but mainly with the wrist. Flick the point downwards and as you do so make a see-sawing action with the hand so that it rises very slightly as the point dips. When you do this the point moves much faster than the hand, enabling it to hit your opponent before he has time to parry.

Practice

Practise the straight thrust to the arm, to the body, to the leg and, of course, to the foot, concentrating on speed and accuracy.

Continue as for foil, adding lunges and footwork. Your lunge will vary in depth according to whether you are attacking the forward target, the main target or the rear target. It is essential when attacking the wrist and hand to lunge only far enough to reach the hand. It is impossible to hit the hand if you lunge too deeply.

THE DISENGAGEMENT

Since you are seldom actually in an engaged position at épée (any more than you are at foil), a disengage can be done in many ways, but it is most often executed against an opponent coming forwards to engage your blade. You can deceive this engagement by disengaging and hitting on the top or side of the arm. There are familiarities with the disengage at foil (*see* Chapter 7) but you will need to use more wristwork in manipulating the épée. As with the straight thrust, you can disengage to the forward target – the hand and the sword arm – or you can disengage underneath the hand, just as you can execute a disengage to the low line at foil. You can do a disengage to the leg or knee as you would a low line attack. It is unlikely that you would do a disengage to the foot as you would have to make some sort of preparation to occupy your opponent's attention. Disengages to the body are also normally performed after preparations of attack. The preparation may take the form of some sort of footwork which ends with a flèche to the body; or, by choosing your time correctly, you might be able to do a disengage to the

The disengage

Fig 59 From the outside position, pass the blade under your opponent's, leading with the point.

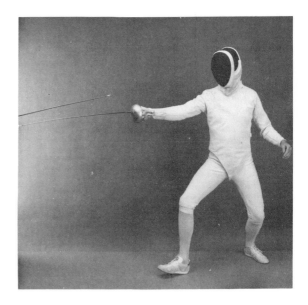

Fig 60 Straighten the arm as you pass under the blade. You may have to use more wrist to manipulate the blade at épée.

body. Either way, the action must be very fast and must not give your opponent an opportunity to hit you on the hand as you come in. Of course, if you are going to the body with a disengage there is nothing to stop you taking the blade with you, so executing a form of prise de fer, which is really like a disengagement in opposition. This is discussed in Chapter 20.

THE CUT-OVER

The cut-over is not a terribly successful way of hitting one's opponent at épée. Although it can sometimes be executed as a form of surprise attack, such as with a flèche, normally the cut-over exposes too much of your own arm to be effective at épée.

THE COUNTER-DISENGAGEMENT

Along with the disengagement, the counter-disengagement is one of the most frequently used attacks at épée. The counter-disengagement deceives your opponent's attempt either to change the engagement or to make a circular parry. At épée it is customary to try to take your opponent's blade and hit while holding it. One of the ways of doing this is to change the engagement and engage the opponent's blade on the other side. Usually this is done in sixte, with the opponent's blade on the outside of your own. As your opponent tries to engage your blade, you can deceive his action with a counter-disengagement, following his blade round until you are clear and able to hit him on the arm. It is also possible to make this attack to the body. In order to hit the body, you have to go past his point, so unless you make the counter-disengagement in opposition you are likely to impale yourself on his point.

The counter-disengage

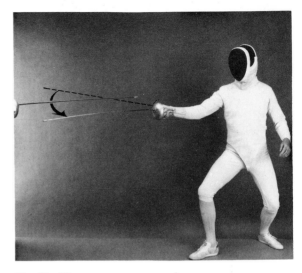

Fig 61 The opponent goes under your blade to engage it on the outside.

Practice

Practise the counter-disengagement attacks on any surface of the arm and then try counter-disengaging with a flèche to the body.

Develop this attack by hitting in opposition. Make this attack on an opponent stepping forward to engage your blade, hitting him on the wrist or hand and moving away very fast.

Make a counter-disengagement, hitting underneath the wrist.

Practise as many forms of this attack as you can think of.

Check List
- Take care to lunge only enough to hit the part of the target you are aiming at.
- If you are attacking the wrist, make a short, very fast lunge. (The shorter you make your lunge, the faster you should be able to move.)
- Ensure that you hit fast and accurately.
- Timing is essential to deceive the blade.

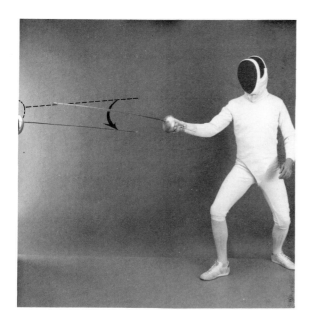

Fig 62   Follow the blade round.

Fig 63   Complete the circle, straightening your arm as you do so, and hit on the wrist.

16 Defensive Actions

One of the interesting things about épée fencing is that you can take or parry the blade with a straight arm, whereas it is not so easy at foil. This is mainly because of the eccentric mounting of the larger guard, which covers the hand more satisfactorily than at foil. In some cases you just deflect the opposing blade with the guard without really taking a parry at all but more often than not you either take a parry and get hold of the blade or take a small parry which deflects the blade. It is a good thing to try to keep your opponent's blade on the outside of your own so that you don't drag his point across the body, as you do when taking a big parry of quarte. The counter-parry of quarte is also very difficult to execute right-hander against right-hander, because as you take the parry your opponent's point passes round your own arm and could easily slip off and hit you. So it is probably best to start by concentrating on taking simple and circular parries of sixte, octave, or perhaps seconde – which is a very strong parry (*see* Chapter 8 on defence). This should be enough to give you a defence against most offensive actions.

USE OF THE GUARD IN DEFENCE

This form of defence is most useful when you have straightened your own arm with your sword well in front of you and your opponent aims to hit you round the arm, hand or wrist. Drop the guard down on top of the foible of the opposing blade and deflect it, riposting immediately to your opponent's arm or body. This is most easily done when your opponent is trying to angulate underneath your hand – just drop the guard and hit to the top of his hand or arm. This action can also be useful against a left-hander who is trying to angulate his point round on to your hand, your arm, or possibly your back. You can use your guard just to deflect the blade.

Practice

Practise with a partner.

Step forwards, straightening your arm, and then lunge to the body. Every so often your partner tries to make an attack on to your wrist. As he does so, just drop the guard on to his blade or to the side to deflect it, riposting immediately to your opponent's body.

Check List
- Ensure that your hand is holding the sword high enough to bring the guard into contact with the foible so that it will block out any target.
- Keep the point under control to make a fast accurate hit.
- Pay especial attention to distance. The big danger is getting too close.

SIMPLE PARRIES OF QUARTE

There are two parry positions of quarte, with variations. The first is the parry which deflects the blade aimed at your wrist or hand. The second is the parry used against an opponent who is coming close to you by flèching or a series of footwork actions and lunging to your body, making it necessary for you to pull your arm right across to what is really a foil parry of quarte (*see* 'The Simple Parry' in Chapter 8: the same principle of opposition of forte against foible applies with the épée).

The first form of parrying quarte is probably the most used of the two. When your opponent attacks to your wrist or hand you need to take a small parry in order not to uncover the arm. Care should be taken not to withdraw the arm. If the point is threatening the top or inside of the wrist, pronate the hand by rotating the forearm, without flexing the wrist, meeting the attacking foible with your own forte and guard, the actual contact being made with the side of the blade, which should lie diagonally across the target, dominating your opponent's blade. The sword arm must not move from the line of the shoulder. This facilitates the way for a direct riposte to your opponent's arm but you may have to resupinate to direct the point successfully.

Fig 65   A simple parry of quarte with the arm pulled well back to protect against an attack to the body.

Practice

Judgement of distance is essential. If your opponent is attacking to the body the first form of this parry will be inadequate.

Time the parry to meet the foible at the very last moment. Do not move the arm more than is necessary; the parry comes primarily from the wrist.

If detaching with the riposte, take care not to put your arm on to a remise (described in Chapter 22). It would be safer to riposte in opposition.

Keep the parry well forward; don't withdraw the arm.

Depending on how close your opponent's body is to you, it may be necessary to pull the arm right back, lifting your point high so

Fig 64   A simple parry of quarte taken forward to protect the wrist and arm.

that you are stopping him forcing his way through – the second form of the simple parry of quarte. The mistake most épéeists make when practising this parry is to riposte immediately. This has the effect of not deflecting the blade as you are riposting before the attack is completed. The most you can hope for in this situation is a double hit, whereas if you pause for a fraction of a second after the parry to make sure that your opponent has gone past your body, and then straighten the arm only enough to reach him, you won't miss him and you won't be subject to a double hit. Close-quarters fencing of this kind has a whole technique of its own at foil, épée and sabre.

Check List

- Parry with opposition of forte to foible.
- You may need a little pronation of the hand to give added strength.
- Raise the point high.
- You may have to twist or move in closer to ensure that the opponent's blade is taken past.
- The riposte may require a withdrawal of the arm first.

Practising Both Parries

Working with a partner from a stationary position, get him to make lunging attacks to the arm and to the body. You must recognise the depth of attack and take the appropriate parry.

Vary your distance by moving sometimes into and sometimes away from the attack. Once you have succeeded in attaining a certain amount of proficiency the whole exercise should be made mobile by the addition of footwork – flèches, ballestras, jumps, and so on.

CIRCULAR PARRIES

The safest circular parry (also referred to as a counter parry) is made in sixte, taking the opponent's blade to the outside of your own and not dragging it across your target. It is usually best at épée to supplement the circular parry by using the wrist in addition to the fingers. The size of the parry will depend on the area to which your opponent is directing his attack and on which parry you choose to take for tactical reasons. For instance, if he is attacking to your wrist you can take a small, circular parry of sixte, possibly with the fingers alone, whereas if he is attacking the upper arm you will need to take a larger parry supplemented by the wrist. If he is going to body or leg, you will need to use the forearm as well. Apart from these differences, the circular parry is the same as for foil. In other words, you gather

The circular parry

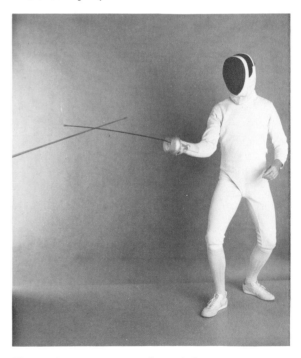

Fig 66 Your opponent will attack from the outside to the inside of your arm.

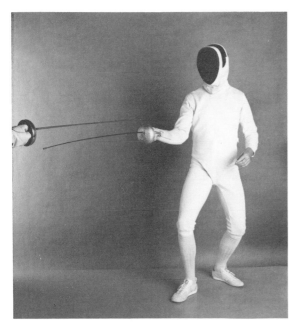

Fig 67 Make a circular movement under your opponent's attacking blade.

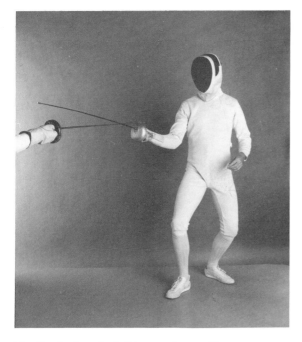

Fig 68 Deflect the foible past the outside of your arm with the forte of your own blade.

the opponent's foible with your forte to kill the attack and not allow it to slip off. This is achieved by a larger circle of the point.

Practice

Start as with the parries of quarte, with a partner lunging at your wrist. Take a circular parry, mainly with the fingers, raising the point very slightly in order to trap the opposing point in your forte. Try not to move the arm or you will expose the outside arm. Experiment by asking your opponent (after he has been parried) to push his blade right in without angulating, to make sure your arm is completely covered. Keep practising this parry until you can accomplish it at speed and cover adequately without moving the hand in or out.

The next progression is for your partner to attack you at the leg, body and upper arm and for you to take circular parries, this time moving the arm as much as is necessary, but still trapping the foible with your own forte on the outside of your blade.

Repeat the exercise with mobility as with the parries of quarte.

Check List
- Parry forte against foible.
- Allow the point to make a slightly larger circle than at foil in order to dominate your opponent's épée.
- Move the arm only as much as is necessary to execute the parry, so as not to expose it.
- Judgement of distance is necessary to select the right form of circular parry.
- Timing is vital.
- The parry should be made at the very last moment.

THE SEMICIRCULAR PARRY OF OCTAVE

The parry of octave at épée is almost identical to the parry of octave at foil, except that if the point is being aimed at your leg you must use the forearm as well as the wrist and fingers, whereas if the attack is coming at the wrist you use only your wrist to parry.

Practice

For attacks coming to the wrist, practise in the same way as for the parry of octave at foil, described in Chapter 8.

Then practise taking large parries to clear attacks to your leg or foot, using the forearm as well as the wrist.

Be careful to time the parry so as to meet the foible with your own forte. This means that you must wait a little longer until the point of the attacking blade is close.

Once you have mastered this parry, add mobility and try stepping in, pulling the arm back as you do so and ensuring that the attacking point passes your arm and body.

Check List
- Keep the hand in three-quarter supination.
- Make sure that you time the parry correctly.
- Take your opponent's foible in your forte.
- You may need to drop your hand if parrying off the foot.

THE SEMICIRCULAR PARRY OF SECONDE

A lot of épéeists use seconde more than they use octave because it is a much stronger parry, since the hand is held in such a way that it stops the opponent from forcing his way through. It is a slightly bigger parry, especially if you are parrying an attack coming to the wrist, so it takes a little longer to execute. Nevertheless, taking the parry in seconde leaves your hand in pronation (palm facing downwards as opposed to a supinated position, in which the fingers are uppermost), which makes an immediate pronated riposte easier than taking time to supinate as you would normally do.

Practice

Let your opponent attack you under the wrist. Starting with your hand in the on guard position, rotate your forearm until your knuckles are pointing to the inside of your own target. Try not to move the arm, and finish at an angle across your target, point in line with your opponent's front knee. As you go over the opposing blade gather it in your forte, holding it firmly underneath your own blade and on the

Fig 69 The semicircular parry of octave. From sixte, describe a semicircle over the opponent's blade, deflecting it with your forte.

Fig 70 The semicircular parry of seconde.
Pronate the hand as you make the parry.

outside of it. Your hand should be above your opponent's point. The pommel will come out of the palm and extend above the wrist.

Manipulating the pommel is a specific skill when taking seconde at foil or épée and necessitates allowing the back fingers to pull the pommel in so that it goes round as you rotate your wrist. Otherwise the wrist jams the pommel whatever grip you use.

Add footwork.

Check List
- The timing is the same as for the parry of octave.
- Parry forte to foible.
- Hold the opposing point in your forte underneath your guard.
- The change from the supinated on guard position to pronated seconde should be done as swiftly as possible. Try not to beat the point but dominate the blade.
- Make sure that you clear the pommel round the wrist.

SUCCESSIVE PARRIES

Parries taken in succession may be the same type or they may be varied. In modern fencing at foil and épée the tendency is not to take more than two parries in succession. If the attack is a progressive one, each feint brings the point in closer until eventually the point is too close to parry.

17 Ripostes

After a successful parry the way is open for the defender to make an offensive action. The parry in épée gives you no right of way as it does at foil. In fact, the épéeist will renew his attack as a form of offensive action or even as a form of defensive riposte. So the riposte has to be much more planned than at foil. Riposting in opposition is probably the safest way of riposting to the body, whilst riposting by detachment is safer if you are going for the hand or arm.

THE RIPOSTE IN OPPOSITION

When you have taken a parry of sixte the opponent's blade will be on the outside of your forte. You can hold the blade in the forte and guard as you move the point on to the opposing target with your riposte. This is a little more difficult to do with a parry of quarte, requiring the arm and the blade to be angled.

Practice

Work with a partner. On his attack to your arm, take a circular parry of sixte, lifting the point very slightly as you do so to keep your opponent's point in your forte and guard. You should now be able to riposte to the top of your opponent's arm, shoulder or head while holding his blade in this position.

If your opponent's hand is high, it would be better to take a parry of octave or seconde, trapping your opponent's foible in your forte and guard and keeping your hand fairly high as you riposte so as to keep his point underneath your guard.

The added benefit of a seconde parry is that you can angulate with the riposte by pushing your hand further to the side and hit on the low left-hand side of your opponent's body.

To riposte in opposition from quarte, take a small parry with the blade well angulated across. Then you can either pronate further, pushing the opposing blade downwards while maintaining contact on top of the blade, or you can move your hand across your body and then change the angle of your blade by pushing your hand out while bringing your point back.

Check List
- A good parry with control of the point is required as the foundation for a good riposte.
- Try to anticipate where you are going to hit with the riposte.
- Decide whether to make an indirect riposte or an opposition riposte.
- Having taken the parry, feel your opponent's foible in your forte. If you lose your opponent's blade you must stop or take another parry.
- Don't forget that your arm or your head may be vulnerable when you make opposition ripostes.

INDIRECT RIPOSTES

Disengagements or counter-disengagements can be used in both the high and the low line. A cut-over is sometimes possible, but only as a surprise tactic since it risks exposing too much arm.

One of the basic épée tactics is the remise – a continuation of the attack in the

Fig 71 The indirect riposte. The finish of the disengage riposte in opposition from quarte, opposing the blade in sixte.

same line (described in Chapter 22) – so indirect ripostes are always a gamble. You must therefore be quite confident that the tactic you are going to use is the right one. Even then, it is safer to finish in opposition rather than by detachment unless you are so close to your opponent that any remise he makes will go past you. An example of this is when you parry octave, closing the distance. Once your opponent's blade has gone past your leg, you are clear to make a disengage riposte, preferably to the body because of the distance. If you took a parry of octave just in front of your foot, on detaching from the blade with your disengagement, you would walk on to your opponent's point.

Practice

On your opponent's attack, step forward with a parry of octave. Once his blade has gone past your body, disengage to your opponent's high line.

On your opponent's attack, take a parry of quarte and, keeping your hand still, disengage under your opponent's blade, straightening your arm in line with your shoulder. You will meet his blade and deflect it with the disengage which you execute in opposition.

On your opponent's attack, parry sixte. He will anticipate a direct riposte and return to guard with a circular parry of sixte. Deceive this parry with a counter-disengagement. You may hit in detachment, underneath his hand and arm, or on the side of his arm, or in opposition by finishing your counter-disengagement in opposition to his blade.

Check List
- If there is any chance of your opponent leaving his point in line, you must finish in opposition.
- Disengagements are done to the high line if the opposing blade is low or to the low line if the opposing blade is high.
- Indirect ripostes are best done with the fingers as they are then smaller, faster and more accurate.

18 Compound Attacks and Ripostes

COMPOUND ATTACKS

Compound attacks are almost identical to those at foil: the feint must travel progressively towards the target before the hit is made with the point. The difference at épée is that because there is a bigger target you can make your feint to the forward target and hit on to the main target. You can make compound attacks to the body, the arm or the leg. Making the feint to the forward target – hand or arm – is a very good tactical move since this occupies the opponent's blade and makes it difficult for him to counter-attack while you are going to the body. Because of the timing element, it is far more usual in épée fencing for a defender to counter-attack – to stop hit or stop hit in opposition – rather than parry and riposte. Whereas counter-attacks at foil must be made to the body, which is the target, at épée, with its larger target, the counter-attack is more likely to be delivered to the forward target – the hand or forearm – while the attack is still reaching for the body.

I will describe one compound attack in detail and you may then adapt for the épée any of those described in Chapter 10.

The One-Two

First of all, decide on the best place to hit your opponent. If you decide to hit on top of the arm, the first feint must be made in order to uncover that area. At foil a small V is made to disengage the blade when attacking with one-twos to the high line, but at épée you have to go round the arm or hit on top of the arm in the high line, so the blade describes more of a semicircular shape or even a complete circle. Apart from that the principle is the same. You make a disengagement to draw a lateral parry and a further disengagement to deceive that parry.

Practice

Work with a partner. Your object is to make a one-two attack, feint to the top of the arm and hit to the top of the arm.

Make your first disengagement from the outside round the inside of the arm. This will draw a simple parry of quarte. Deceive this parry with a circular action underneath the blade to the top of the arm.

Make the attack progressive, with the point travelling forwards. Take care not to lock the arm straight with the feint. Complete the straightening of the arm as you deceive the parry. When going to the arm, make a shorter lunge or you will be too close and miss. The blade action is effected with the fingers supplemented by the wrist. The point describes a helix and the hit is made with the fingers. The point should arrive before the front foot lands.

To make a one-two with feint to the arm and hit to the body, make your first feint as before, but preferably going from the inside to the outside of the arm, drawing a parry of sixte which will open the inside for an attack to the body. As you deceive the parry of sixte, accelerate your lunge to reach the body as quickly as possible.

To make a one-two with feint to the outside arm and hit to the leg or foot, make your first feint high to the top outside of the arm, enticing your opponent to lift his hand even further as he parries, which will open the way for your hit to the thigh, knee or foot.

The compound attack at épée can be executed with absence of blade – that is, avoiding contact with the opposing blade all the way to the target; or it could start in absence and finish in opposition, or vice versa.

Counter-disengagements, executed either as a feint or as a trompement (deception of the parry), are very useful in compound attacks at épée. Épéeists like to keep their outside arm covered so they seek to either take the blade or change the engagement to

The one-two to the wrist

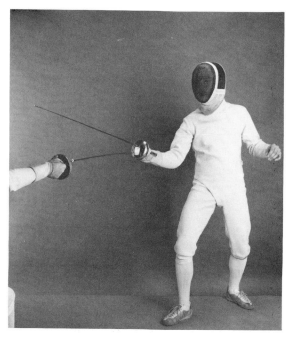

Fig 73 Disengage under the blade and feint to the outside arm.

Fig 72 Your opponent (right) is covering his inside line.

Fig 74 As your opponent attempts to parry the feint, disengage round it and hit the inside wrist.

keep the opposing blade on the outside of their own. The counter-disengagement can be used to deceive either the change of engagement or the circular parry.

After practising these attacks, add mobility and then modify the rest of the foil compound attacks as above.

Check List

- Make sure that your feint draws the required parry by making it convincing enough to be taken for an attack.
- Manipulate the blade with your fingers as much as possible.
- Modify the length of your lunge according to the area of the target you are aiming for.
- Make the attack progressive and vary the timing.
- Be aware that the opponent may not parry but may execute a counter-attack. This is sometimes brought about by an opponent who is less experienced and hasn't the tactical knowledge to do anything except stick out his arm.

COMPOUND RIPOSTES

These are similar to the compound attacks except that they are preceded by a successful parry.

An épéeist's basic tactic is to remise after the attack. This makes compound ripostes very dangerous to use. It is essential, therefore, to draw the opponent's blade with the first feint. It is also safer to finish in opposition.

Distance dictates where you hit your opponent and this is affected by whether he lunges and recovers, steps back after he recovers, or flèches with his attack. You can adjust your own distance by either stepping back, jumping back, or stepping forward with the parry. Your riposte can then be delivered without a lunge, or with a lunge, a step-forward lunge or a flèche. Whether you finish in opposition or detachment depends on the distance.

Any of the compound ripostes at foil may be adapted for épée. There is more scope in épée because of the larger target, which means that you can make a feint at one depth and finish at another – for example, a feint to the forward target with the hit on the main target.

Use any of the foil compound ripostes and finish in opposition.

Practice

On your opponent's attack, step back and take a parry. As your opponent recovers to guard, riposte with a one-two, finishing in opposition.

If taking a circular parry of sixte, make your disengagement to the inside of the arm and then disengage in the opposite direction, hitting in opposition to the top of the arm.

Try making the riposte with a double or a counter-disengage–disengage according to the way your opponent recovers.

Check List

- Select your compound riposte carefully, preferably finishing covered.
- Make the blade movements progressive.
- Manipulate the blade with the fingers so as to make the ripostes fast and accurate.
- If doing footwork with the riposte, ensure that the feint draws the blade.
- Start your compound riposte after your opponent has begun to recover.

FREE PLAY

Now introduce the strokes you have learned so far into the competitive situation of free play.

1 In order to learn épée distance, which is so important, you will need a partner. Start at lunging distance – the distance you must

cover in order to reach your opponent's hand with a lunge. Decide who will attack and who will defend, swapping roles occasionally. As you both move backwards and forwards, the attacker tries to gain an advantageous distance in which to hit the arm or the body. The defender uses one parry only, either simple or circular, using direct ripostes in opposition or detachment.

2 Start as above. The attacker now tries to anticipate the defender's parry and attempts to deceive it with compound attacks. The defender may take two or more successive parries – identical or varied – to try to pick up the compound attack.

3 The attacker this time tries to induce a particular parry on which he makes a compound attack. To do this, you must (if you are the attacker) observe your opponent's reaction to the various feints and false attacks you make. You will soon realise that opponents react in certain ways to given signals. You can use this to your own advantage: give a signal to which you have discovered the answer, and you exploit it to secure the hit.

19 Counter-Attacks

Since the épée is not a conventional weapon there are no rights of way as there are at foil, and if you can hit your opponent within $\frac{1}{25}$ second of his hitting you a double hit is recorded. Counter-attacks (which are offensive actions into offensive actions) are used, if not to gain a single hit, to force a double hit.

Counter-attacks at foil are described in Chapter 13; read the section again to refresh your mind. At all three weapons, you must first be sure that the counter-attack is the right tactic and then commit yourself totally to the hit – otherwise you will not succeed. Even with the épée, when double hits are possible, the object of a stop hit is to arrest the attack.

THE STOP HIT

The stop hit is an offensive action into an attack. You disregard the attack from your opponent and attack into it. Unless you are convinced that you can hit your opponent without him hitting you, take into account the possibility of a double hit: if it would lose you the fight the stop hit may be the wrong choice.

If your opponent is attacking to your body, hitting him on the wrist may have the effect of arresting his further movement forwards so that only your stop hit lands; alternatively, you could move away very quickly after the hit so that his attack doesn't reach you.

If a double hit is all you require to win the bout, no matter what target your opponent is attacking you can attack into it. If you do so with enough conviction, you may cause him to hesitate with his attack as he realises the consequences of a double hit, and you might well hit without being hit.

Practice

Your opponent attacks you to the body. As he starts his attack, reach out without lunging and hit him on the hand or forearm. Your rear foot should be clearing the ground with a step back as the hit arrives, but take care not to move back before you actually make the hit.

A very successful way of executing a stop hit is to slip off the opponent's blade as he pushes it through in opposition to the body, disengage, hit him on the forearm and move your body away as quickly as possible. This latter type of stop hit must not be confused with an attack on the preparation, in which you hit your opponent whilst he is in the process of making a preparation of attack. (If you tried a stop hit on the preparation of attack, your opponent would not engage your blade).

Once you have developed the speed and accuracy of hitting with the stop hit, add mobility and execute the stop hit with as many variations of footwork as possible, including the flèche.

Check List
- Choose the correct stop hit wisely.
- When you are convinced the stop hit you have selected will be successful, execute it with complete conviction.
- Manipulate the blade with the minimum amount of body movement so that your counter-attack takes your opponent completely by surprise.
- Accuracy of hitting is important for if you miss you will be hit by the attack.

- Judgement of distance is also important.
- Do not move away from the opponent until you have made the hit.

THE STOP HIT IN OPPOSITION

As with the stop hit, you must remember that this is an attack, albeit an offensive-defensive action. You must anticipate the final line of your opponent's attack and close it whilst hitting him with the counter-attack. With such a movement, there should be no fear of a double hit. It is therefore safer than a stop hit.

Practice

Start as with the stop hit, your opponent attacking to your body on the inside of your blade. As he does so, execute a disengage attack into it. Take care to keep the hand fairly high, pushing your point through in order to close the line into which your opponent is attacking, with the opposition your own forte to his foible. This counter-attack, like the stop hit, must start almost at the inception of your opponent's attack or he will finish up dominating your blade instead of vice versa.

This counter-attack can be executed in any line, provided you can remain covered whilst performing it. The two outside lines of sixte and octave are the most favoured.

Check List
- You must attack with conviction and not approach this stroke as a defensive one.

Fig 75 The stop hit in opposition to the foot. With your opponent's blade held in the forte of your own, hit the toe.

- You must start right at the beginning of your opponent's attack.
- Do not swing the arm but keep it covered behind your guard.
- Use fingers and wrist to make the movement fine enough to give speed of execution and strength in opposition at the same time.
- As this is an attack, the point must start travelling to the target from the second you start, otherwise your action will become a parry and riposte.

20 Takings of the Blade
(Prises de Fer)

A natural instinct for an épéeist is to remise (see Chapter 21). This being so, one must have a way of dealing with renewals of attack, whether they be remises, redoublements or reprises. One answer is to take the blade. Bear in mind that at épée it is possible to parry as well as take the blade with a straight arm, which is not possible at foil.

There are various shades of prises de fer at épée which are not so clearly defined as at foil. For instance, whereas at foil one can make a disengagement with absence of blade, at épée it is possible to make disengagements going down the blade, in the form of a graze, a froissement, a taking of the blade, or simply as an attack in opposition.

ATTACKS IN OPPOSITION

An attack in opposition starts as an ordinary attack as described for foil, but finishes with the attacker pushing his blade through his opponent's, taking the opposing blade out of line as he does so, maintaining contact with it and dominating it.

Try the simplest of these attacks first. Make a disengage attack to the high line of sixte over your opponent's sword arm, pushing his blade, which may be covering the target, to one side as you make the hit.

Another example is to hit in opposition in octave. Move your blade over your opponent's in the direction of the octave position, once again pushing your opponent's blade to one side forcefully as you hit the target. It is best to go for the leg or the thigh rather than the foot: an épéeist will almost certainly pull his foot out of the way and avoid your blade to hit you on the hand while you are travelling the long distance to that target.

All the prises de fer can be executed with a straight arm at épée. Quite often an épéeist will step forwards straightening his arm as he takes the blade; or he may in fact already have his arm straight and follow up with a further step forwards, a lunge, or a flèche. This is easier to do at épée because of the larger guard and the eccentric mounting of the blade – the advantage is that you don't uncover your arm while taking the prise de fer.

Practice

Practise the attacks in opposition as described above on your opponent's bent arm in the on guard position.

Practise the same attacks on his straight arm, this time hitting to the wrist or arm. Now add mobility, moving backwards and forwards. The attacker attacks through to the body with attacks in opposition; when his opponent straightens his arm, he makes the same attack to the hand or arm.

Check List
- Feel of the blade is essential as you must be sure that you have the blade and can maintain dominance throughout the attack. It may be necessary to raise the point slightly as with the parries.
- Judgement of distance is important as this will indicate what part of the target you are able to hit.

- Speed of execution, giving you the element of surprise, is important.
- Lead with the hand and not the foot.
- The danger point is just before you actually take the blade as this is when your opponent is most likely to deceive.

THE ENVELOPMENT

The envelopment is fully described in Chapter 13. The difference at épée is that the special blade presentation required at foil in order to hit the target is not necessary, because the larger target allows you to hit on top of the arm or the shoulder and also the head, so you can usually make a successful envelopment irrespective of the height of the hand. It is safer done in sixte or octave. The envelopment may be executed with a bent arm or a straight arm, but is best done on your opponent's straight arm.

Fig 76   The envelopment. Having engaged your opponent's blade in your forte, using the wrist, completely circle the blade and hit in opposition on the arm.

Practice

Use the practice examples given in Chapter 13 for foil but practise taking the blade with a straight arm as well as a bent one.

Check List
- As for foil, but with especial attention to dominating the blade forte to foible and using the wrist only.

THE CROISÉ

As this attack takes the blade from the high line to the low line on the same side, at foil it is safest to make it in quarte. At épée, however, it would be dangerous to take the blade in a foil quarte, though you could achieve it by taking a shallow parry of quarte and rotating your wrist into a seconde as you go to the low line so as not to lose the blade.

This stroke is very efficient against a left-hander, taking the blade from the high line of sixte and hitting either on the outside of your opponent's arm, or to his body or back under his sword arm, or to his forward thigh or leg.

Practice

Practise with your opponent holding his sword in his left hand – unless you are fortunate enough to have a left-hander to practise with.

Make your croisé from the sixte side to octave and hit on the leg or thigh.

Try the same attack, hitting on the outside of the arm.

Against a right-handed fencer, take his blade in a shallow parry of quarte and, by rotating the wrist to seconde, hit him in the low line of the body.

Add footwork.

Try the croisé with a straight arm as well as a bent arm.

Check List
- Make sure that you have domination of the blade when executing the croisé.
- Check the techniques for this stroke listed in Chapter 13.

THE BIND

The bind is a very large taking of the blade and therefore has limitations at épée. First, it is safer done with a bent arm rather than a straight arm, so you must be that much closer to execute it successfully, which means that you must hit to the body.

Because taking the blade diagonally across the target from the high to opposite low line or vice versa means taking your opponent's point right across your own target and arm, complete domination of his blade is required. In order to maintain this domination and not allow your opponent the opportunity of slipping off your blade, you may need to close the distance while executing this stroke.

Practice

As for foil (Chapter 13), adding changes of distance as above.

Check List
- As for foil.

21 Defence against Takings of the Blade

If your opponent has engaged your blade and is about to make a prise de fer, probably one of the easiest ways to defend against this is to take either an opposition parry or a ceding parry. There is a difference between parrying with opposition against a prise de fer and the normal parry with opposition.

OPPOSITION PARRIES

When your opponent has engaged your blade and is taking a prise de fer attack, the easiest defence is to oppose the final thrust of his attack. As most prises de fer are taken on the outside of your blade over your sword arm, you oppose this final thrust in a parry position of sixte. In this instance your opponent has sought out and engaged your blade as part of the preparation of his attack. As he transports your blade with his to make his hit on your target, close out the final thrust of the attacking blade with your forte. If his thrust is made into the octave line, close the attack out with an opposition parry of octave.

Practice

Start with your arm straight and your point threatening the opposing target. Invite your opponent to take either an envelopment or an opposition attack in sixte. Allow him to complete the prise de fer and at the very end, as he pushes his blade through, oppose in sixte, forte to foible.

If the blade is coming in very high, rotate your hand slightly, knuckles innermost, point high (position of tierce), and once again oppose the final thrust of the point. This is a slightly stronger opposition.

Start again, with your opponent enveloping into the octave line; take an opposition parry of octave or seconde.

The last two will serve to defend against a croisé done from the high line of quarte to underneath the arm.

Check List
- Timing is essential for this stroke.
- Take the opposition parry at the last moment.
- Ensure that you are opposing your forte against the attacker's foible.
- Keep your point under control in order to make a riposte.

THE CEDING PARRY

Épéeists often take prises de fer or attacks in opposition on the outside of the blade in order to provoke an opposition parry in sixte, which they will deceive with a disengage. Foilists also use this tactic. It is therefore safer to take ceding parries. Start by bending the arm and partially 'giving way' before taking the parry, usually in another line.

Practice

To time this parry it is best to start with your opponent making his attack in opposition in

Fig 77 A ceding parry of prime. Note the height of the hand and the opposition of forte against foible.

the sixte line. As he pushes his blade down your blade, you will feel a tendency for your point to drop downwards. Allow the point to drop but, as you do so, lift and pronate your hand, rolling your point underneath your opponent's. Lift your arm up, keeping the point down, and transport the attacking blade across your target high on to the quarte side, keeping your guard above the blade.

Now get your opponent to make an envelopment straight thrust. Do exactly as above, but you must start the ceding parry after the envelopment and as your opponent pushes the point forwards for the straight thrust.

Check List
- Time the start of the ceding parry to coincide with the final thrust of the attack, bending your arm as you give way.
- Oppose forte to foible.
- Keep contact with the blade while making the parry.

DECEIVING THE PRISE DE FER

Takings of the blade can be deceived in two ways. The first is to deceive the actual engagement at the beginning of the prise de fer by disengagement or counter-disengagement. The second – a much more subtle method – is to allow your opponent actually to engage your blade and finish his prise de fer, and, as he is doing so, to move away, slip off his blade and hit him on the wrist or hand. This is a true épée stroke; the conventions involved make it invalid at foil.

Practice

Deceiving the initial engagement is basic fencing and relatively easy to do but the ability to slip off the blade after it has been engaged and subjected to a prise de fer requires hours of practice.

22 Renewals of Attack

As the name implies, these attacks are continuations of an offensive action after the initial attack has missed, failed, or been parried. How they are executed depends on your opponent's defensive action or actions – whether or not he ripostes and whether he steps back.

There are three renewals of attack: the remise, when the attack is renewed in the same line; the redoublement, when you renew the attack with an additional blade or arm action; and the reprise, when you renew the attack while going through the on guard position.

A renewal of attack at épée can be used against a riposte in preference to a parry.

THE REMISE

The remise is a continuation of attack in the same line. The épéeist, having made an unsuccessful attack at the hand, can renew the attack by passing from the arm to the body without changing the line. The conventions do not allow this to be done in the same way at foil.

This renewal could also be redirected to the original area of attack, especially if your opponent is riposting.

Practice

Make a straight thrust to your opponent's wrist. When he parries a small parry of quarte, remise through to the upper arm or body. This may entail increasing the lunge or flèching.

This time, your opponent takes a circular parry of sixte and makes a direct riposte to

the outside of your arm. As he does so, you remise to the top of his arm, thus blocking out his riposte. If you lunge with your attack, you can keep your arm straight as you recover and allow him to impale himself on your point.

If your opponent takes a large parry of quarte and detaches from your blade with the riposte, you can remise by leaving your arm in line as you recover and block out his riposte.

Check List
- Select your renewal of attack according to your opponent's defensive actions.
- Keep your point in line with the target after having made the attack.
- Try to resist pushing your point forwards whilst recovering but allow your opponent to run on to it.
- If you are doing this as a defensive action make sure that your arm is covered behind your guard as you remise.

THE REDOUBLEMENT

The redoublement is most often performed against a direct riposte since it has the same effect as a stop hit in opposition (described in Chapter 19). It is the renewal of an attack with an additional blade or arm movement.

If, after parrying your attack, the defender does not riposte, you can renew your attack by disengagement or counter-disengagement, in either opposition or detachment.

Practice

Make an attack high to the outside of your opponent's arm. As he parries a circular parry of sixte, redouble by disengagement under the hand or inside the hand.

Make an attack to the outside of his arm. Redouble by disengagement to the leading foot.

This time, when you make your attack your opponent parries quarte. As he ripostes with a direct riposte, return to guard with a straight arm, making a disengagement in opposition to the top of his arm, deflecting his blade as you do so.

Check List

- Keep your arm straight as you recover with your redoublement.
- Use a little wrist to supplement the hand, especially when redoubling against a riposte.
- Adjust your distance accordingly, if necessary stepping back after your recovery. If redoubling into a riposte, time it so that the forte finishes up opposing the foible.

THE REPRISE

The reprise is a renewal of attack by going through the on guard position. It is used a great deal at épée since making a short attack immediately followed by a fast renewal by flèche is a very good tactical ploy.

The foil-style reprise – a lunge followed by a recover forwards followed by a further lunge – is basically too slow (for foil too these days). However, a form of reprise is sometimes performed at épée by means of what is called a 'réassemblement'. A réassemblement is when, having recovered from a lunge, you slide the front foot back towards your rear foot, raising yourself on your toes as you do so. At épée this gives you an acute angle down on to the wrist.

The reprise

Fig 78   Attack with a lunge.

Fig 79   Recover forwards by bringing the rear foot up into the on guard position.

Fig 80   Re-lunge or flèche, keeping the arm straight throughout.

Practice

Make an attack at your opponent and, when he takes a circular parry of sixte, jump into the on guard position with both feet, landing on the balls of the feet, and flèche with a disengagement to the body.

Make an attack to the arm. As your opponent takes a circular parry of sixte and ripostes with a lunge, return to guard, slide your front foot backwards and stand up, reprising by disengagement to his front wrist.

Check List

- When you reprise forwards, the point must precede the foot at all times.
- If recovering to make a flèche, jump on to the balls of the feet, using this bounding action to increase the speed of the flèche.
- The réassemblement action should move your leg backwards out of reach of your opponent's blade as you go up on to your toes.
- The reprise must be done fast in order to catch your opponent by surprise.

These renewals may also be performed effectively at foil.

23 Observations on Épée Tactics

Epée tactics are dictated by the fact that the whole body is the target and that the guard must be used as much as possible to cover the extremities of the target such as the forward arm and leg. To use the guard successfully, you must pay attention to the line of fence – the imaginary line running through your rear heel and front foot and your opponent's front foot and rear heel. In this on guard position your forearm should be hidden behind the guard, so the only target open to your opponent is your body. In order to hit your forearm he would have to angulate his blade round your guard, leaving his own forearm open to your point. If he attacks your body, he runs the risk of going past your point with his arm. So, to attack, épéeists usually take the blade, which solves both these problems. If they don't take the blade with their attack, it is best if they take shortish but very fast lunges or flèches to the forward target or body.

To defend against a taking of the blade you can slip off it, hit your opponent and move away before his point reaches your target, or you can completely avoid his taking of the blade and hit him while he is trying to find the blade.

If you fail with an offensive action, it is far safer and quicker to keep the arm straight and renew the attack in opposition rather than go forwards or backwards with a parry. When you bend your arm to make a parry, you expose that arm to a hit, whereas when you keep your arm straight your forearm is covered behind your guard. If you don't renew the attack, it is better to parry with a straight arm than to bend the arm in defence. Usually the opponent's riposte can be read, so it is possible to choose one's renewal.

The parry is the safest form of defence when you are not sure of your opponent's true intentions – particularly if, as you advance towards your opponent with a particular offensive action in mind, he attacks you on that preparation. As you are not to know whether his attack is simple or compound, or whether it is aimed for the forward target or main target, it is best to parry with a bent arm and completely dominate your opponent's blade before deciding on a further response.

Épéeists are generally tall and well built and corps à corps (bodily contact) is permissible, so you need a firm grip on your épée to deflect the blade of an opponent who is much larger and stronger than yourself. You also need to be able to fence at close quarters in order to deal with the fencer who closes in on you. If there is a height difference it is sometimes advantageous to the shorter of the two fencers to close distance in defence rather than open the distance. This puts the taller fencer with the longer arm at a disadvantage. Difference in height also affects the speed of the lunge: the smaller the fencer, the faster the footwork and lunge; the taller the fencer, the longer the reach and the slower the footwork and lunge.

Your best route to success is to find a good fencing coach who will improve your techniques and advise you tactically, and then to practise against épéeists better than yourself and make use of their tactical advice.

Fig 81 Annette Campbell versus Alda Milner-Barry in the Ladies
Épée Championships in London, 1986.

PART FOUR
THE SABRE

24 Characteristics of Sabre Fencing

The sabre is a cutting weapon as well as being a pointed weapon and for this reason it differs markedly in shape from the foil and the épée. Points are scored at sabre both by hits made with the point and by cuts. A cut is made by striking the target with a part of the blade other than the point in such a way that the blow is strong enough to be seen clearly as a cut and not a 'lay on' of the blade, and is forceful enough to produce a certain amount of sound. The blow should never be so hard that it would hurt the opponent through his protective clothing. The cut may be a through cut, which is a slicing action, or it may be a dry cut, which is a single blow. The action of the cut may be delivered by the wrist or from the elbow. The cut delivered from the elbow – molinello, a windmill action – comes in rather heavily and strongly and is apt to hurt, so most strokes or through cuts should be done with the wrist, which renders them more effective and faster, with less power.

The sabre target is everything above the line formed by the crease where the legs join the trunk when a fencer is sitting down on guard. The jacket normally worn by a sabreur does not incorporate a cuissard (the extension that goes down to the V of the groin between the legs); it is short and just covers the target.

The sabre blade is unlike that of the foil and épée. It has no button. It is flatter and the point is folded back on itself to form a small loop which allows it to be used to make cutting actions, so you can make hits with the point and also cuts with any side of the blade. The guard of the sabre wraps round the hand to protect it from the opponent.

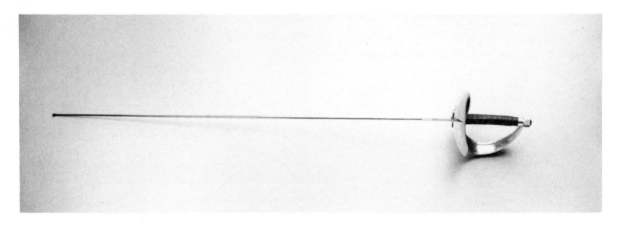

Fig 82 The sabre. Note the wrap-around guard to protect the hand.

THE CONVENTIONS

Like foil, the sabre is a conventional weapon; there is a right of way. The right of way is given to the attacker who initially straightens his arm and continuously threatens the target with the point or the cutting edge. When the threat is made with the cutting edge, the blade and arm must form an obtuse angle of about 135 degrees.

It is more difficult to distinguish the right of way at sabre because, although the arm starts moving first, it doesn't straighten quite so fast as with a thrusting weapon. Nevertheless, the president, in deciding who has right of way, is looking for the first person to start straightening his arm.

As with the épée, there is a forward target – the sword hand and arm. Whilst the guard gives a certain amount of cover to the hand provided the sabre is held the right way, the arm is still quite vulnerable to an attack or counter-attack.

Most attacks made with a sabre are made as cuts rather than points, so the blade approaches the target at an angle. For this reason defending at sabre is very difficult unless you can anticipate where the attack is to be directed. So at sabre you try to completely avoid the opponent's blade when attacking and to find the opposing blade when defending. Note also that when beating your opponent's blade you must beat in the middle or foible of the blade and not into the guard: if two hits arrive at the same time as a result of beating into the forte or guard a parry and riposte would be scored against you.

HOW TO HOLD THE SABRE

Study the photograph. The sabre is held at a much more perpendicular angle than the foil and épée, which are thrusting weapons and held as an extension of the arm. As the sabre is a cutting weapon it should be held in such

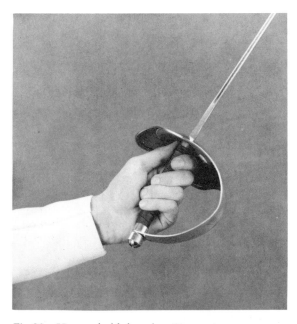

Fig 83 How to hold the sabre. Your grip must enable you to make cuts and defend against them.

a way that the sabreur can make cuts and defend against cuts.

Place the grip (the handle) in your sword hand so that the cutting edge of the blade is on the opposite plane to the thumb, which actually touches the grip only by the first phalange. Wrap your remaining fingers around the grip so that the tips of the fingers rest on the inside plane. There should be a gap between the base of the thumb and the grip.

THE ON GUARD POSITION

The on guard position described in Chapter 3 is the same for all three weapons except for the position of the arms. At sabre, both arms are target and they should be held in such a way that they can be defended and covered.

Place the back of the fingers of your rear arm on the rear hip so that both arm and hand are well out of the way of your opponent. The hand need not stay here as it

Fig 84 On guard. The back arm is needed for balance. It is a good habit to place it on your back hip, as described.

is important to use it for balance, just as with the other two weapons, but returning to this position is a good habit to acquire.

The front arm, the sword arm, should be held with the cutting edge and guard facing directly towards the opponent, with the point slightly in front of the hand and the blade at approximately 45 degrees. Your hand should be held very slightly below the elbow, which should just brush the forward hip, and the forearm should be roughly parallel to the ground. The sword should be carried and not just held and the sword arm and shoulder should be completely relaxed. This is called the 'offensive–defensive' position.

25 Cuts

THE DRY CUT

The main method of making a hit at sabre is with the dry cut, so it must be practised diligently in order to make it fast and light. Unfortunately, in the heat of battle one sometimes gets a little close or overexcited and when this happens the tendency is to hit too hard. To be a good sabreur you must practise and practise the cut so that this does not happen. It must be a percussive action that just detaches from the target and should not be a 'dead', heavy blow that stays in contact. Many sabreurs make the mistake of intentionally pulling the blade off after a head cut instead of allowing the blade to rebound.

The cut is best executed by a flexing of the wrist, sometimes supplemented by the fingers. The blade is presented to the area of the target to be cut – that is to say, the cutting edge is brought into line with that area – and by flexing the wrist a cut is made.

The main areas for cutting on the body are the flank (the side of the body underneath the sword arm); the cheeks (right and left); the head (on top of the mask); the chest (from the shoulder down as far as the midriff on the inside of the sword arm), and the belly (the area between the midriff and the lower limit of the target). The same cuts can be made to the forward target: the cut to the head or the top of the arm; the cut to the flank on the outside of the arm; and the cut to the chest or belly on the inside of the arm. It is also possible to cut upwards underneath the arm or wrist.

Practice

It is obviously best to practise with a partner but if this is not possible hook a mask on to a wallbar or the back of a high chair roughly at the height of a head when in the on guard position. Then position yourself so that you can just reach the mask with the last inch of your blade without lunging. You are now in a position to make a cut to the head.

Straighten your arm very loosely without locking the elbow so that the blade is 10–12 cm above the mask. Then, by flexing the wrist, just cut the mask with the cutting edge of the sabre. You should hear a crisp tap but the blow should not be so forceful as to make the mask move.

Practise this a few times and then make it into one complete action, delivering the cut while you are still straightening the arm. Concentrate all the time on making a clear, clean tapping action and not a heavy blow.

Once you have succeeded in doing this, change the area of the cut. As your arm goes forward, rotate your forearm to cut the right side of the mask (cheek), then the left side (cheek) while rotating your forearm the other way. Concentrate on making the straightening of the arm and the cut into one smooth action.

If you can find a suitable surface such as a punchbag, you can practise cuts to the body. The mechanics are exactly the same, but the hand might be slightly lower – though never lower than your opponent's chest.

When you make any of these cuts, whether to mask or body, your hand should finish immediately in front of your forward shoulder and should not be allowed to swing across the target which would expose it to a stop cut (described later). So hits to the top of the arm or the head finish with the blade angulated.

Check List
- The hand must travel forwards before the cut.
- The cut must be controlled from the wrist in order not to hit too hard.
- The presentation of the blade – that is to say, the aiming of the cutting edge – must be done while the arm is straightening.
- The cut should be heard but at the same time should not be too forceful.
- The cut should be made with the first 2–4 cm of the blade.
- Do not move the hand out of line with the shoulder.
- Avoid dropping or lifting the hand while making simple attacks.

THE THROUGH CUT

This cut is made with a circular action and the side – that is, the flat – of the blade is used so that as you make the cut it can be pulled through and back to the original starting point.

Through cuts are usually made to the chest, the inside arm, or by back cut to the flank, the outside arm or the cheek (the opponent's right cheek). The cutting action should be neither too light, in which case it would not come through properly, nor too heavy, which would be crude and painful for the opponent.

Practice

I will describe the through cut to chest as it is executed against an opponent, but in the early stages, before you have acquired the skill, the repetition needed would cause him pain, and it is best to practise on a suitable substitute such as a punchbag. When you do practise against a partner in the later stages,

A through cut to the chest

Fig 85 Present the side of the blade to the chest.

Fig 86 Make a circular action with the wrist, striking the chest with the flat side of the blade.

Fig 87 The circular action of the cut is made large enough to go around the opponent's arm and return to the offensive–defensive position.

make sure that he is wearing a sabre underplastron.

Stand at riposting distance and, while straightening your arm, make a circular action with your wrist, contacting the target with the side of your blade high near your opponent's left clavicle. Pull the cut across and diagonally downwards so that it goes underneath your opponent's arm, which is in the offensive–defensive position, and finally resume your own offensive–defensive position.

A back cut to the flank or cheek is usually executed as a riposte, as a counter-attack, or possibly as part of a compound attack, since it is necessary to attack on the outside of your opponent's blade.

Make a disengage under your opponent's blade, using the wrist, and then make a slicing cut up under your opponent's sword arm to his flank. It may be necessary to drop the hand slightly to achieve the desired angle.

The same cut may be used for the outside arm or cheek.

Check List
- The cut should come solely from the wrist.
- The cut through to the chest should start and finish in the same position.
- Avoid swinging the arm, especially with the through cut to the flank.
- The cut must be made with the last couple of centimetres of the blade.

26 Simple Attacks

Simple attacks are less easy to define at sabre than they are at foil and épée. This is because sabre is fenced very much in absence of blade and what is a direct attack and what an indirect attack is not totally clear. For instance, I could make a direct attack at my opponent's right cheek, but if I execute the same action but finish at flank it is not at all clear whether I have performed a cut-over and therefore an indirect attack or a direct attack to flank. In practical terms, however, the complexities of sabre terminology are of little importance.

Sabre attacks with the point are usually made as attacks on the preparation or possibly counter-attacks, and these are described in Chapter 34. To hit with the point at sabre, you must turn your hand fully into pronation, the knuckles uppermost, so that the flat of the blade may bend in order to make the hit.

DIRECT ATTACKS

The Direct Attack with the Point

To make a hit with the point, straighten the arm as for foil but, as you do so, pronate the hand so as to hit with the point before the front foot lands. You should make this attack to the body as it is unlikely that you will be able to hit the arm.

Practice

Practise with a partner, both adopting the offensive–defensive position of tierce at a distance where one may reach the other to the body with the point. The attacking fencer, dropping the point and lifting the hand – and at the same time straightening the arm and rotating the forearm so that the hand is in pronation – steps forwards and hits his opponent at chest with the point.

All these movements must be combined into one smooth action. The hand and arm must be moving slightly before the foot but all will finish together.

Having successfully executed this attack with a step forward repeat the action with a lunge, with a step-forward–lunge, and with a flèche, opening up the distance as necessary.

With both fencers moving, select the attack according to the distance.

Note that with the electric sabre the point

Fig 88   A point thrust or lunge.

must be travelling forwards as you make the hit for it to register.

Check List

- Do not lift the hand too high. It must be below the shoulder. Pronate fully.
- The blade presentation and arm action should become one smooth movement. In order to gain the right of way, the arm must be straightening and the point continuously threatening the valid target.

The Cut to the Head and the Top of the Arm

The only difference between these two cuts is the depth of the attack.

The cut has already been described but to make it into an attack it must be delivered to the target. The most usual way of doing this is to step with the cut, lunge with the cut, or

A cut to the head

Fig 89   The blade is presented with the cutting edge to the head. Note the angle of the blade.

Fig 90   Hit with the last couple of centimetres of the blade, hand in line with the shoulder, guard level with the opponent's solar plexus.

flèche with the cut. Quite often at sabre the lunge is done more as a large step with a drag of the back foot rather than as a true lunge.

Practice

Working with a partner, present and straighten the arm to the opponent's forearm and as you do so step forwards with your front foot, making the cut as the front foot lands. Keep your hand in line with your shoulder so that the cut angles round your opponent's guard. You must move in a little closer in order to allow for this angulation.

Now make the same action, with a lunge to the head.

Repeat with a step-forward–lunge to head.

Each repetition should be faster than the one before until the action is as fast as you can make it.

Check List

- Remember to straighten the arm with the hand fractionally ahead of the foot.

- Keep the hand in line with the shoulder so that the blade is angulated towards the head or top of the arm.
- The arm must move smoothly, directly to the target area it is going to hit.
- If stepping forwards, remember to move on to the heel first and lunge immediately the rear foot hits the ground.
- There should be an acceleration between the step and the lunge.
- Remember that if you are flèching the hit must arrive before or as the back foot hits the ground.
- If flèching, avoid twisting your shoulder inwards.

The Direct Attack to the Chest or the Belly

This attack, although it is direct, does entail changing the direction of the cutting edge and some people would call it an indirect attack if made from the offensive–defensive position of tierce. But, as it doesn't really change the line, I group it with direct attacks.

As you start the arm straightening, rotate the forearm to present the cutting edge to the chest and make the cut as described before.

Having made your cut at the chest, you may now rotate your forearm a little further so as to make the cut horizontal to the opponent's target, the belly.

Practise as for the cut to the head or the top of the arm.

INDIRECT ATTACKS

The Cut to the Flank

As you start your attack, rotate your forearm and direct your cutting edge underneath your opponent's arm. As you do so you will go over the top of his blade, making a cut-over. Having directed the cutting edge to the flank, make the cut with the wrist as already described.

You can also make an indirect attack by disengagement, either with a cut or with the point. To execute a disengagement to the flank, as you drop your point underneath your opponent's blade, rotate your forearm so that your hand is pronated and make the cut horizontally to your opponent's target – the flank.

Practice

Start moving your hand forwards, at the same time rotating your forearm so that your blade goes over the top of your opponent's blade, making a cut low to the flank (just above the target line).

Now make this attack with a step forwards, making the hit as the front foot hits the ground.

Then make a disengage attack to the flank, dropping your point underneath your

Fig 91 The cut to the flank. Rotate your forearm as you attack, directing the cut to the flank. Use the same action to cut to the cheek.

opponent's and describing a semi-circle with your blade, rotating your forearm as you do so to present the cutting edge low to the flank.

Do this with a step forwards. Now with a partner, execute both of these actions with a step forwards, a step forwards and lunge, a flèche, and a step forwards and flèche.

Check List
- The hand must move smoothly with the cut, the straightening of the arm and the cut being one movement.
- Cuts to the flank should be made as low as possible to avoid the opponent's arm and make it more difficult for him to parry.

- As you cut to flank, you can make the cut upwards underneath your opponent's arm, so as to go underneath what would normally be an adequate parry.
- As with the direct attacks, do not move the arm out of line with the shoulder.

There are other simple indirect attacks but they depend on what guard the opponent is adopting. Your blade must go either underneath it with the disengagement or over the top of it with a cut-over.

It is sometimes possible to execute a counter-disengagement at sabre but this is usually done as an attack on the preparation and finishes on the arm.

27 Defence

Defence at sabre is very difficult as the attacks can be made with front-edge cuts, back-edge cuts and cuts through with the side edge as well as hits with the point. In order to parry, one really has to anticipate the final line of the opponent's attack or develop very fast reactions.

THE FIRST DEFENSIVE TRIANGLE

The parries are split into two basic groups: those which defend against cuts coming upwards (prime and seconde) and those which defend against attacks coming downwards (tierce and quarte). Each of these has as its apex the parry of quinte.

Practice

The parry of prime is executed against an attack being made upward towards your belly. First rotate the forearm completely until the point of your sabre is pointing towards the ground. Move your hand across the target, finishing with the hand cheek-high and the point slightly forward. Your guard should be at the same angle as the cutting

The first defensive triangle

Fig 92   Prime.

Fig 93   Seconde.

Fig 94 Quinte.

Fig 95 Tierce.

blade so that the blade is parried up into the forte and guard.

From prime it is easy to move to seconde. This parries attacks coming upwards to your flank. Move the hand across the target, lowering it slightly to chest height, with your point ahead of the guard and pointing at the opponent's thigh.

Practise the transition from the offensive-defensive position of tierce to the parry position of prime and seconde. Once you have mastered this, ask an opponent to attack you, both to belly and flank, with a cutting upward action.

THE SECOND DEFENSIVE TRIANGLE

This defensive triangle defends against cuts coming downwards at the target and it comprises the parries of tierce and quarte. To

Fig 96 Quarte.

111

Fig 97   Quinte.

take tierce, pull the arm back further than the offensive–defensive position, flexing the wrist so that the guard is pointing towards the cutting edge which is attacking your outside arm or flank, the blade leaning out slightly past the guard. This will gather the opposing blade into your forte and guard.

To take quarte, swing your hand across the target, keeping your elbow stationary and dropping the hand very slightly to the level of the hip, with the guard in front of your fist and your hand in line with your forearm.

Practice

Move from offensive–defensive to either tierce or quarte. Make the transition smooth and fast. Then get your opponent to attack you to the flank and the chest and use the parries of quarte and tierce.

THE PARRY OF QUINTE

This parry is the apex to both defensive triangles. It parries attacks coming down on top of the head.

Practice

From the offensive–defensive position of tierce, lift the hand straight up, rotating the forearm so that the cutting edge of your sabre is almost parallel to your head. The hand should be slightly above the head and to the right side, immediately above the elbow, which should be in line with the shoulder. The thumb should be underneath the grip, the wrap-around portion of the guard over the hand and the latter just in front of the head. The point of the sabre should be just above the level of the hand.

Practise moving from tierce to this position smoothly and fast, then get your opponent to lunge to your head and practise parrying the cut to the head.

Check List
- Ensure that your thumb is behind your opponent's cutting edge.
- Parry forte to foible with the guard covering your hand.
- Timing of parries is very important. If you take them too soon, they will be deceived; if you take them too late, you will miss.
- Try to vary your parries as much as possible to confuse your opponent.
- Do not go out to meet the attacking blade but stop at the parry position.
- Limit the arm movement to the minimum.

CIRCULAR PARRIES

Many parries may be executed in a circular fashion but the two most useful are the circular parry of quinte and the circular parry of tierce.

The circular parry of quinte can be taken at a later stage than the simple parry of quinte, so it is a very useful reaction parry. The circular parry of tierce can be a fast defensive action to attacks to the hand or arm, and can also be quite a large sweeping action, picking up most attacks to the body.

The Circular Parry of Quinte

Practice

Practise with an opponent. As he attacks to your head, step forward with a circular parry of quinte. This is done from the offensive–defensive position by dropping the point and circling it back up underneath your opponent's blade and lifting the hand to a position of quinte (the hand immediately above the elbow).

The Circular Parry of Tierce

Practice

On your opponent's cut to the inside arm, make a circular action underneath your opponent's blade using your wrist, parrying forte to foible and turning the cutting edge outwards as you finish.

Practise taking this parry to any attack your opponent makes to your body. The circular action must be enlarged and possibly even supplemented with forearm in order to engage the blade forte to foible in a tierce parry position.

Check List
- These circular actions must be executed smoothly and fast. This means that the size of the circle depends on the area of the attack.
- Circular quinte is executed as you are lifting your hand up.
- Circular tierce may be done with the arm still or while the arm is moving.
- Parry forte to foible.

113

28 Ripostes

As the right of way is the same as at foil, finding the opponent's blade with a successful parry opens the way for the riposte. Ripostes may be simple direct, simple indirect, or compound and they may be delivered with any form of footwork, including a flèche. The direct ripostes are from tierce to head, from quarte to cheek or head, from quinte to flank, from seconde to cheek, and from prime to flank. Indirect ripostes, like indirect attacks, are not clearly definable but the following actions are among the most usual: tierce, cut to chest by cut-over or disengagement; quarte, cut to flank either as a front-edge cut or a back cut, again by disengagement or cut-over; and quinte, cut to head by cut-over.

DIRECT RIPOSTES

Practice

Having made a successful parry of tierce, as you straighten your arm to make the riposte, present your cutting edge to the top of the head, remembering to keep the arm in line with the shoulder and not swing it across, so that as you cut the blade is at a diagonal angle to the arm.

Having made a successful parry of quarte, as you straighten your arm to make the riposte, rotate the forearm, presenting the cutting edge to the cheek, and return to the offensive–defensive position.

Having made a successful parry of quinte, rotate the fist forwards slightly, while dropping the hand horizontal to the floor. Straighten your arm and cut to the flank. Return to the offensive–defensive position.

Having made a successful parry of seconde, as you straighten your arm to make the riposte, rotate your forearm, presenting the blade and cutting to the cheek. Return to the offensive–defensive position.

Having made a successful parry of prime, as you straighten your arm, rotate the forearm and drop the hand, making a cut to the flank. Return to the offensive–defensive position.

SIMPLE INDIRECT RIPOSTES

Practice

Having made a successful parry of quinte, make a cut-over over your opponent's blade by swinging your wrist and forearm to present your blade and cut to the head. Keep your hand immediately above your elbow while doing this. Return to the offensive-defensive position.

Having made a successful parry of tierce, make a cut-over over your opponent's blade, rotating the wrist and forearm and cutting to the chest. Return to the offensive–defensive position.

Having made a successful parry of quarte, make a cut-over over your opponent's blade, rotating your wrist and forearm as you do so and either cutting with the front edge or making a through cut with the back side of the blade to the flank. Return to the offensive–defensive position.

Try all your indirect attacks as indirect ripostes. Time your ripostes to coincide with your opponent's return to guard or parry. All these ripostes should be practised with a variety of footwork, using the full length of the piste.

Check List (for all ripostes)
- Remember that the foundation to a good riposte is a sound parry.
- Present the blade smoothly as you make the riposte.
- Try to riposte into an opening line.
- Keep your hand and guard immediately

in front of your arm, which should be an extension of your shoulder.
- Do not swing your arm across your body.
- Wherever possible, cut with the last couple of centimetres of the blade.
- Judge distance carefully before making the riposte so that you can decide on the appropriate footwork; without a lunge, with a lunge or even with a flèche.

29 Footwork as Preparations of Attack

Partly as a result of modern sabre tactics, certain types of footwork are more applicable to the sabre than to the other two weapons.

THE CROSS-OVER

The cross-over is similar to a light, fast run. Unlike a running action, however, you should not lean forwards. Your head and trunk should remain upright. The action is used as a preparation on an opponent who is retreating very fast away from you down the piste.

The cross-over is used in conjunction with many other varieties of footwork but seldom alone. Sometimes a cross-over lunge is used; sometimes the cross-over is preceded by a step forwards or a ballestra, finishing with perhaps a flèche.

It is important to remember that the cross-over is a preparation. Keeping this in mind helps you with the timing of an attack.

The cross-over

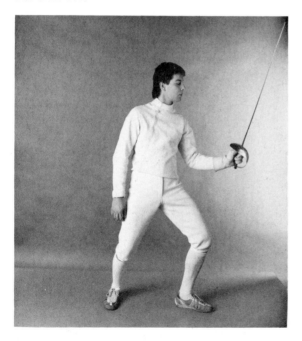

Fig 98   From the on guard position, move your back foot forwards.

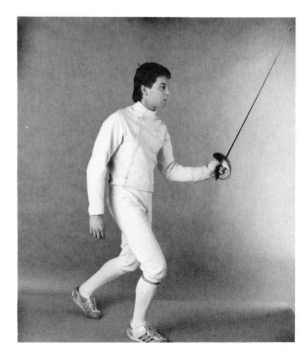

Fig 99   The back foot passes the front foot.

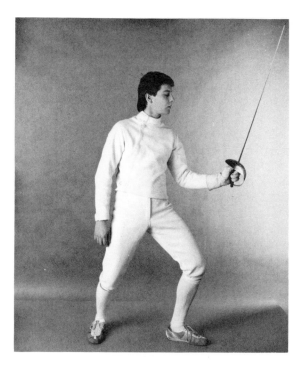

Fig 100 Bring your feet back to the original position by a further movement forwards.

Practice

From an on guard position, bring your rear foot past your front foot with a running motion, landing with the toe forward. The front foot, which is now the rear foot, is brought through in the same running action and, as its heel hits the ground, the rear foot swivels to the former on guard position. This completes one cross-over.

You may do as many cross-overs as you wish, keeping the line of fence, but remember that while doing so you are open to a counter-attack or an attack on the preparation.

The movement is very similar to a flèche attack, but the flèche is a method of delivering an attack whereas the cross-over is purely a preparation until such time as you straighten the arm. It is then bound by the same ruling as the flèche: the hit must arrive

when the rear foot hits the ground. Practise this with various combinations of footwork: step forward, cross-over; cross-over flèche; step forward, three cross-overs, step, cut.

Check List

- Keep your head up and maintain your balance as you may have to change direction or stop very rapidly.
- The feet should make small but very fast movements.
- Keep the line of fence.
- Lead with the toes (this is not essential but makes a smoother and more natural running action).
- When you stop the cross-over action, you should have your feet at right angles in the normal on guard position.

THE LUNGE AT SABRE

The standard lunge described in Chapter 3 is used by sabreurs but they also use a step as a method of delivering the attack as well as a

Fig 101 The sabre lunge.

form of lunge which is best described as halfway between a lunge and a step.

Practice

Practise with an opponent. Step forwards with a cut to the head. The cut should arrive as the front foot hits the ground.

Now increase the distance the front foot travels to that of a lunge, but instead of leaving the back foot stationary allow it to drag along the ground so that you finish in the on guard position. This form of lunge is very good if you want to flèche with a renewal or if you wish to make a false attack in order to parry and flèche with your counter-riposte.

Check List

- Judge the distance well so as to be able to reach your opponent.
- Keep your balance throughout.
- Allow the rear foot to be dragged forward.
- Finish with your weight between your two feet so that you are balanced in order to use any other form of footwork.

THE RUN BACKWARDS

The run backwards is used when your opponent is closing on you rapidly and you feel that you are unable to defend yourself. It is a purely defensive action.

It is also possible to make a cross-over backward – both movements are very similar – but I prefer the run.

It is not good tactics to make either a cross-over backwards or a run backwards against an opponent's cross-over forwards – he might well catch you wrong-footed.

Practice

There is no special technique. As the name implies, it is simply a matter of running back

The run backwards

Fig 102   From the on guard position, move the front foot first.

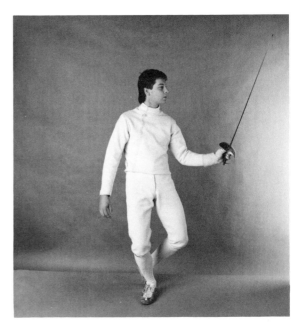

Fig 103   The front foot passes the back foot.

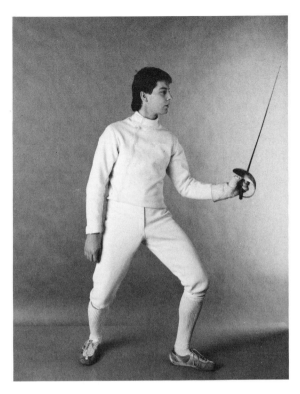

Fig 104   Continue moving backwards to
the original position.

as fast as you possibly can. Needless to say,
you must not turn your back on your
opponent: run backwards while facing him.

Check List
- This should be a very fast and balanced
  movement.

30 Elementary Tactics

The best way to start sabre fencing is to practise wall exercises. One fencer stands with his back foot touching the wall so that he is unable to move backwards. His partner adopts lunging distance and marks the position of his own rear foot. Most fencers drag their foot slightly when they lunge, and the faster your lunge the more it will drag, so allow for the drag when you mark the position of the back foot.

The attacking fencer starts with simple direct and indirect attacks. His opponent tries to parry these and riposte. It is best to work on a fixed number of attacks so that you can mark the success of the attacks or the ripostes.

At the start of this exercise, the attacker will be guessing where he thinks his opponent will parry and the defender will also be trying to guess the attacker's intentions. The more you concentrate, the more you will develop your perception.

After practising against the wall, use a full 14-metre strip. Starting at one end, the attacker will advance down the piste using different types of footwork and finishing with a simple attack. Once again, his partner, who is keeping fencing distance with him, must try and parry the attack.

Reverse the roles, travelling down the piste in the opposite direction.

The next stage of this exercise is for the defending fencer to attack whenever he thinks the distance will allow it. This is now a free-play situation: either fencer may attack. As many different strokes as possible should be brought into play.

31 Compound Attacks

Compound attacks are attacks which include one or more feints. Some can be executed with the point as at foil and épée, but at sabre it is much better to use the cutting edge for compound attacks. Remember, you may go over the blade with a cut-over, under the blade with a disengagement, or around the blade with a counter-disengagement – and the cuts may be made with any part of the blade. This offers a very wide variety of compound attacks.

A compound attack of two movements comprises a feint to provoke your opponent into a parry and a trompement to deceive the parry. To be successful, the feint must draw a parry and the trompement must cleanly deceive the parry, for the rules are that the right of way is lost if the blade is found during a compound attack.

FEINT AT HEAD, CUT TO FLANK

This is probably rather an obvious attack, although most sabreurs use it at some time or another. The object is to provoke the opponent into taking a parry of quinte by threatening with a cut at the head, and then to deceive the parry and rotate the blade down to a cut at flank.

A compound attack: feint to the chest, and cut to the head

Fig 105   Feint to the chest.

Fig 106   Cut-over the attempted parry of quarte.

Fig 107   Cut to the head.

Practice

Working with a partner, position yourself at riposting distance and make a cut to the head. Stop the blade just short of the head. As your opponent lifts his hand from tierce to quinte, deceive it by rotating round the outside of the blade – achieved by rotating the forearm – then cut to flank.

In order to perfect the timing of the deception, start by separating the movement into three. (1) Straighten your arm and hold the feint just above your opponent's head (the blade must be held at an angle of about 135 degrees). (2) Your opponent lifts his blade up to quinte (as his blade is travelling up, yours must be travelling down). All that is needed to achieve this is a rotation of the forearm – the blade is already at the correct angle to go over and round the arm. (3) Make the cut.

Now repeat (1) and then join (2) and (3) together, concentrating on a fast, crisp action.

Now execute the whole exercise with a lunge. Hold the feint fractionally, then accelerate through to the cut.

Repeat this with a lunge, then add variations of footwork (Chapter 29).

Check List
- Do not straighten the arm completely or lock the elbow and shoulder with the first feint.
- Accelerate the trompement.
- Maintain the hand at the same level, neither lifting nor dropping it.
- Avoid swinging the arm. Keep it in line with the shoulder. This is very important when executing a flèche.
- Make sure that you cut cleanly with the cutting edge.

FEINT TO FLANK, FEINT TO CHEST, CUT TO FLANK

This attack incorporates two feints but the principle is much the same. Half-straighten the arm with the first feint, straighten it three-quarters with the second feint, and finish straightening it with the cut.

It would be best to accompany this attack with more than one foot movement.

Step forwards, feint to flank, lunge with the feint to chest, and cut to flank.

Practice

The feint to flank is made by turning the forearm in order to present the blade to that area. This must be done whilst straightening the arm. By rotating your forearm in the opposite direction, you will feint to chest. Then turn the forearm back to make the final cut to flank.

The attack starts with the arm moving forwards, followed by the step-forward lunge. The movement must accelerate through so that you are going much faster when you make the cut than when you start the attack. At all stages of this compound attack your blade should move in an opposite direction to that of your opponent, changing direction every time his does.

Work with a partner. The defender steps back with a parry of tierce (moving from the offensive–defensive position to a low parry of tierce) whilst the attacker is stepping forwards with the feint and lunging with the second feint and cut.

Check List

- Make your feints by just rotating the forearm.
- Don't swing the arm.
- Accelerate from beginning to end.
- Ensure that you avoid your opponent's blade completely by going over it.
- Move your feet fast and keep perfect balance.
- When making combinations of footwork, use momentum to help with acceleration.

FEINT TO OUTSIDE ARM, DISENGAGE TO HEAD

This is an example of a compound attack using a disengagement. The disengagement is a slightly smaller action than the cut-over so it may catch your opponent unawares. The action must be made with the wrist only – not the arm – which requires a lot of practice.

Practice

Working with a partner, practise just disengaging, only using the wrist, from the inside to the outside of the arm and then from the outside to the inside of the arm or the head. The wrist describes a complete circle, with a rotation of the forearm at the very last moment to perform the cut – the arm must not swing.

Now use this action in a compound attack. With a partner, make a cut-over feint to the outside arm, disengage under and cut to the head. As with all the compound attacks, the hand goes slightly before the foot, irrespective of what method is used to deliver the attack – whether you step forward, lunge or flèche. This cut can be delivered in any area as a through cut with either side of the blade.

Check List

- The hand must precede the foot and, as with the other compound attacks, the hit must arrive as the foot lands.
- The trompement must completely deceive the blade.
- Do not swing the arm.
- The disengagement must come purely from the wrist.
- The method of delivery and any footwork used must accelerate towards the completion of the attack.

32 Successive Parries

One answer to a compound attack is to take two or more parries in succession. Any of the parries described in Chapter 27 can be used in combination as successive parries.

Parry Quinte and Seconde, or Parry Quinte and Tierce

Defence against a feint to the head, cut to the flank.

Parry Quarte and Tierce

Defence against a feint to the chest, cut to the flank.

Parry Tierce and Prime

Defence against a feint to the flank, cut to the belly.

Parry Seconde and Quinte

Defence against a feint to the flank, cut to the head.

Parry Tierce and Circular Parry of Tierce

Defence against a feint to the outside arm, cut to the inside arm.

Parry Quinte, Seconde, Quinte

Defence against a feint to the head, feint to the flank, cut to the head.

Practice

The combination of single parries you choose to make in succession will depend on the type of cut and attacking action your opponent makes. The parry of quinte and seconde is usually an easier reaction parry to take against an opponent attacking at head and flank, although, if you can anticipate head and flank, it is probably much safer to parry quinte and tierce.

It is possible at sabre to use what are called feint parries. This is a tactical method of making your opponent finish his attack in a known line, so successive parries may comprise one or more incomplete parries – feint parries – and the final parry, which stops the attack.

Compound attacks involving the head are probably some of the most difficult to parry as the defensive blade action has to travel to the extremes of the target.

Check List
- Move smoothly from one parry to the next.
- Don't come out to meet the blade but wait for it to arrive in your parry.
- Remember to parry forte to foible.
- Don't riposte until you have found the blade.
- Wherever possible, premeditate your successive parries.

33 Preparations of Attack

Preparations of attack by means of footwork are described in Chapter 29. In this chapter I shall consider preparations by attacking the blade and preparations by taking the blade. Because of the very nature of the weapon, which employs a cutting action, attacking the blade – by a beat or the execution of a froissement down the blade – is much easier at sabre than taking the blade.

ATTACKS ON THE BLADE

Beat Attacks

You can make a beat on your opponent's blade with any part of your own blade – that is to say, with the sides, with the cutting edge, or the back edge – but obviously a beat with the front edge is much stronger because of the way the weapon is held. If the beat is done as more of a deflecting action it is probably best done with the cutting edge, whereas if it is purely a preparation to cause your opponent to react then the side beat is just as effective. For example, if you are attacking to your opponent's right cheek, it would probably be better to make a side beat and then go straight in to the cheek whereas, if you are approaching your opponent fast and his point is threatening you, then it would be better to make a stronger beat with the cutting edge to remove his blade from its line.

One of the most important things about the beat is the point of contact on the opposing blade. The rule is quite specific when it says in Article 420 paragraph 2: 'In an attack by beating on the blade, when the beat is made on the forte of the opponent's blade, i.e. the one third of the blade nearest the guard, the attack is badly executed and the beat gives the opponent the right to an immediate riposte.' According to this rule a beat into the forte would constitute a parry by your opponent. Apart from this very important rule involving the right of way, just as at foil and épée, if you want your opponent to respond to the beat, it is better to make it on the foible.

Whilst the beat can be used as an offensive–defensive action, it is really not a

Fig 108 Beating the blade. A stronger beat is produced by beating with the cutting edge. The beat detaches, making it an attack on the blade (attaque au fer).

true defensive action in that sense. With a parry, it is necessary to move your hand across the target so as not only to deflect the opposing blade but to catch the foible in your own forte. With a beat attack, it is best not to move your arm but to make the beat from the wrist, with as little movement of the forearm as possible. By doing it this way you reveal less of your own forward target for your opponent to stop-cut and your preparation is much more of a surprise since you are not telegraphing your intentions to your opponent. Obviously, the attack you make after a beat can be direct, indirect or compound.

Practice

Come on guard with an opponent, with both of you in an offensive–defensive position of tierce. Start the practice at riposting distance. As the attacker, turn your wrist inwards and simultaneously straighten your arm; as you do so beat your opponent's blade on top with your cutting edge. Your sword will now be diagonally across your body. Try not to move your arm sideways more than is necessary. Make a crisp, bouncing type of beat with a flexing of the wrist at the end of the extension. Your opponent's blade should move under the impact of the beat but the impact should not be so strong as to knock the sword out of his hand: you may not hit your opponent after he has been disarmed. Allow your beat to come off your opponent's blade as though it were a springboard, presenting your blade as it goes to the target.

For your first practice it would probably be better to beat on top of the blade and hit on top of the arm just over the guard. Then try beating on top of the blade and hitting on the upper arm; then beating on top of the blade and cutting to the right cheek; then beating on top of the blade and cutting to the head.

To practise the skill of beating, it would probably be best to beat and cut to the forearm, beat and cut to the upper arm, beat and cut to the cheek and beat and cut to the head as a rhythmic exercise. Once you have mastered that, step forwards with each of the beats. After that you can vary the combinations of footwork: step forward and hit; step forward, lunge and hit; and step forward, flèche and hit.

A very effective way of executing a beat attack at sabre is to change the engagement first. We call these change-beats. By going underneath your opponent's blade you can beat it on the outside, then, as before, go directly to the target; or go underneath, beat the blade on the outside, and then make the attack by cut-over. The change in direction between the beat and the cut will confuse your opponent.

Practise making a side beat to the inside of the blade and cutting to the cheek. See how fast you can make this. Listen to the rhythm of your beat and cut and see whether you can speed it up.

Make a side beat on the inside of your opponent's blade and make a cut-over to his outside arm or flank.

When you have practised these beats standing, try making them with a variation of footwork, stepping with the beat and lunging, flèching, or executing a ballestra with the attack.

Check List
- Make the beat crisp and from the wrist, trying not to move the arm more than necessary.
- Make the beat as though you are hitting a springboard, bouncing off to the target.
- Present the cutting edge of your blade from the beat.
- Make sure that you beat the foible and not the forte.
- Try to come forwards as you are beating rather than beating first and then following with the attack.

The Pressure

The pressure can be used at sabre, though the opportunities compared with foil and épée are very limited because at sabre most actions are executed with absence of blade. A pressure is usually best done on the inside of the opponent's blade, and if you step forwards and engage with the side of the blade and give the pressure almost immediately, your opponent's reaction will probably be against the pressure – he will push back. Once again, your attack may be direct, indirect or compound.

Practice

Step forwards, engaging your opponent's blade with the side of your own, foible to foible. Don't move your arm across as you do so; use the wrist only to make this engagement. Immediately make a pressure, which should move the opponent's blade and tend to startle him slightly. Then go for an immediate cut to the forearm.

Now step forwards and engage the blade on the inside. Make a pressure and cut to the head. The cut may be executed with a lunge or a flèche.

Check List

- Engage foible to foible without moving the arm.
- Make the pressure foible to foible without moving the arm.
- The pressure should be a quick, surprise action.
- Present the blade immediately on making the pressure.
- The pressure may be much more of a downward movement and in order to accomplish this, instead of pressing the blade sideways, keeping the arm in line with the shoulder, apply the pressure to the top of the blade.

TAKINGS OF THE BLADE

Takings of the blade, or prises de fer, are frequently misunderstood by sabre fencers. This happens because referees quite often confuse takings of the blade with attacks on the blade. Any preparation of attack which makes contact with the opposing blade seems to be referred to as a taking of the blade.

The interpretation of a prise de fer at sabre is the same as at foil and épée (see Chapters 13 and 20): you transport your opponent's blade in one direction or another, preferably holding it clear of your own target as you hit. Sabre technique makes this very difficult to accomplish. To make a prise de fer, as with a pressure, you must engage the blade first. Of course, an engagement is a prise de fer but when done at sabre it becomes an integral part of whatever prise de fer you are making, whereas at foil and épée the taking of the blade is a quite separate action from the actual attack. As the prise de fer action is made coming forwards, it is very difficult to attack on this preparation at sabre, whereas at foil it is relatively easy.

Because the prise de fer requires an engagement at the outset, it can at first sight look like an attack on the blade and this, to my mind, is where the misconception arises. The criterion is whether the blade is transported out of line or just beaten or pushed, as in the case of an attack on the blade.

At sabre, obviously, you cannot make a bind or envelopment as you can at foil. The foil is a pointed weapon and according to the rule you must hit with the point travelling forwards which enables you to achieve a different angle when engaging forte to foible, allowing domination of the blade with the wrist. At sabre, the domination when making a prise de fer is effected more with the forearm than the wrist and the final attack can be made as a cut or as a hit with the point.

A classic prise de fer at sabre is to take the blade with a circular parry of tierce and riposte to the head while holding the opponent's foible in your forte. It can look very similar to a change-beat in tierce with a cut to the head. In fact the distinction is of little importance to the president, who has to judge only as to right of way. It is, however, important that students of fencing, fencing masters and learners understand clearly that there is a difference between the two actions.

Prime to Head

This is very useful against an opponent who has his point in line. Alternatively, if you are coming forwards fast, you can sometimes pick up your opponent's blade with a parry of prime on his cut to the chest.

Step forwards and engage the opponent's foible in your forte in the position of prime. Rotate your blade back into the tierce position. As you do so, keeping the opponent's blade in your forte, pass your blade under his, transporting his blade across to a

Fig 110   Circle your blade up under your opponent's to tierce.

Fig 109   Engage the opponent's 'straight arm point feint' in a forward prime.

Fig 111   Continue the circle in the same direction and cut to head. Note how your opponent's blade is transported from a point in line to a parry position of tierce. This is a true prise de fer at sabre.

covered position of tierce. You may now cut to the head (a direct attack) or cut to the flank (an indirect attack). Prises de fer may be followed by direct, indirect or compound attacks.

Practice

Start your practice with your opponent's point in line, threatening your target. As you take your prime, move your hand slightly forwards and continue this forward movement as you transport the opposing blade to tierce. As you make your cut, your hand should be in line with your shoulder. When you feel this action is going smoothly and successfully, practise coming forwards with a cross-over or step-forward preparation. Your opponent, who is stepping backwards at this stage, selects his moment to make a point attack, to which you take your prime to head prise de fer.

Seconde to Chest or Belly

This is an alternative prise de fer to prime to head and may be made against an opponent who is threatening you with his point.

Step forwards, take your opponent's blade in seconde and rotate your wrist very slightly so as to cut with the side of the blade back across his belly. If you are going to his chest, lift your hand slightly in the seconde and once again cut with the side of the blade, but this time to the chest.

Practice

Start with your opponent's blade in line. Take seconde, ensuring that you collect his foible in your forte. Straighten your arm, carrying your opponent's blade with you, and make a clean cut with the side of the blade to the belly.

Now change the direction of this cut to the chest. This will necessitate lifting the hand slightly higher as you take seconde so as to

keep your opponent's foible in your forte. The cutting action is still executed with the side of the blade, but slightly downwards. When you have mastered this technique, practise as above with your opponent attacking on your preparation.

Tierce to Head

This prise de fer may be taken either on a straight arm or, if you are at close quarters, on a bent arm. It is very similar to a parry of tierce and riposte. The difference is that you maintain contact with the blade and you travel forwards to find your opponent's blade with the prise de fer.

Take a circular parry of tierce, holding your opponent's foible in your forte, and riposte in opposition to the head.

Practice

Start as with the other prises de fer with your opponent's point in line threatening your target. Engage the blade in tierce, straightening your arm as you do so, and cut to the head.

Now practise the same action without your opponent's sword being in line. With your opponent on guard in the offensive-defensive position of tierce, step rapidly forwards without straightening your arm, engage his blade in tierce and cut, using the wrist only. This variation sometimes results from a rapid closing of distance, or it may be executed if your opponent closes the distance instead of retreating while you are on the lunge.

Check List (all prises de fer)
- Ensure that you engage your opponent's foible in your forte.
- Transport his blade out of line and either maintain contact as you cut or, if you detach, do so in such a way that his blade is deflected.
- Straighten the arm as you make the prise

de fer (unlike foil) so as to maintain opposition.

- Decide how far you must straighten your arm in order to make the cut.
- Pay particular attention to footwork so that you are balanced and in a position to make a prise de fer.

I have selected three clearly defined prises de fer as examples for you to practise. I have named them according to where they start and finish, but of course they may be executed as direct, indirect or compound actions, and there are many more variations. Try out as many variations as possible until you arrive at the ones you feel happiest with.

Remember: a prise de fer at sabre must transport the blade.

34 Counter-Attacks

Counter-attacks are described in Chapter 13 for foil and in Chapter 19 for épée. They are attacks made into your opponent's offensive action. If they are attacks made into an attack, they are called 'stop hits' or 'stop cuts' at sabre and to be in time they must arrive a period of fencing time before the final movement. If they are attacks into other forms of offensive action, then they become just pure counter-attacks. Stop hits are therefore counter-attacks but counter-attacks are not necessarily stop hits. A lot of stop cuts are executed to the forward arm as this is the first part of the opponent's target presented to you as he makes an attack; attacks into the preparation or ordinary counter-attacks which do not involve an attack from your opponent can sometimes be made to the body. The head is often very vulnerable to a counter-attack as, instead of keeping themselves upright, fencers tend to move the head forwards as they advance, which brings it within range of a very fast counter-attack.

STOP CUT UNDER THE WRIST

As your opponent attacks you to the head, drop your hand down, rotating your forearm so that the cutting edge is uppermost and the blade laterally across the body. Straighten your arm and cut under your opponent's wrist. To be in time, the stop cut must precede the attack by one period of fencing time.

So, because the cut to the head is a simple attack, after the stop cut you must either parry the attack or step back and avoid it: if both hits arrive the stop cut will be given 'out of time'.

Practice

Get an opponent to step forwards and lunge to your head. As he steps forwards, drop your hand and cut up underneath his guard to his wrist. When you can do this on his step forward (an attack on the preparation), change your timing so that you make the cut as he starts his lunge. At sabre it is usually safer to make a parry at the end of your counter-attack in case the attack comes through. It is safer still to move away from the attack so as to give yourself more time and a larger safety margin.

So once you have succeeded in stop cutting your opponent underneath the wrist practise moving back immediately after the cut. This means clearing your rear foot from the ground and either jumping back or moving back very rapidly with either a cross-over or a step back as you make your cut underneath the wrist. Get your partner to finish his attack to your head so that you can put a parry and riposte on to the end of your action.

A lot of practice needs to go into the timing of the stop cuts so that you can make your stop cut and remove your body well away from the attack.

Now stop cut your opponent as he comes forwards and jump right out of distance of his attack. You must ask your partner to come through slowly with a step forward and a lunge to your head, and let him make a full lunge – not too fast to start with. You do not parry this and he should not even contact your blade. You should be able to jump right out clear of the attack. Keep practising this and gradually let your partner speed up his attack until you can do this without him hitting you at all. Then, and only then, if he comes in close enough, will you need to parry and riposte. If you can move your body away fast enough, obviously, you don't need to parry and riposte.

You have learned to make simple and compound attacks to all parts of the arm and body and stop cuts are really only these same attacks made into an attack. So you should now practise making all the simple and compound attacks into counter-attacks. Give less time to compound counter-attacks as they are rarely successful. It is sufficient to know that they are possible.

Stop hits are not very often made to the body at sabre as this would entail closing the distance too much and you would run the risk of being hit with the attack. Some counter attacks may finish to the body, though this is rare.

Check List (all counter-attacks)

- The stop hit must arrive a period of fencing time before the final movement of the attack. It is preferable, therefore, to cause your opponent's attack to fall short by avoiding it completely.
- Make sure you hit clearly so that if judging is being done visually your hit can be seen distinctly.
- If using the point to make a stop hit, ensure that you hit clearly before your opponent.
- Do not lean or step forwards with the stop cut as this will slow down your ability to open the distance.

35 Observations on Sabre Tactics

Sabre is fenced totally in absence of blade. This means it is far easier to attack than defend. The attacker also has the advantage of being able to vary his footwork or method of delivering the attack, which alters the timing of his offensive actions. When attacking at sabre, the hand starts to move at almost the same time as the foot, which makes it very difficult for the president to see who initiates an attack. If one fencer advances down the piste, his opponent has the option either of retiring or parrying, or of attacking into his opponent's offensive action. The fencer advancing will immediately make his attack as soon as he senses that an attack is about to be launched. It is then up to the president to decide which fencer started straightening his arm first and therefore has the right of way. Most sabre fencers, when retiring, will launch attacks preceded either by an attack on the blade or a taking of the blade in order to ensure that they have the right of way.

To overcome the difficulty in defence you must try to use 'second intention' defensive actions, for example making feint parries in order to persuade your opponent that you will be opening a particular line. If this tactic is successful, you will know exactly which part of your target your opponent is going to attack and you will not only have time to take the appropriate defensive action but ample time to select the most suitable riposte.

If your opponent is advancing rapidly towards you with cross-overs you must decide whether you can attack on his preparation, parry the attack and riposte, or whether it would be better to break distance – that is, to run back to the end of the piste. If you wish to parry and riposte or attack, you must use fast steps back; do not try to cross-over, which might catch you on the wrong foot to be able to lunge or parry and riposte.

Simultaneous actions are not allowed at sabre. If they occur, the president awards a right of way by the toss of a coin. After a hit is scored, this 'right' is passed to the other fencer. Sabre fencers use this rule to their own advantage. For example, if you have the advantage, it is worth counter-attacking your opponent at the start of his attack in order to force a simultaneous action, from which you will be awarded the hit. Clearly your opponent will be aware that this might be your tactic and he may make some form of offensive action in order to draw your counter-attack and parry and riposte. Both of you now have to be very, very cunning. It is possible to start an attack with a lunge and parry the counter-attack in mid-lunge. This is especially effective if you close the distance so that your riposte is made at close quarters.

Remember: the best tactics of all are those that are the simplest and end with you hitting and not being hit.

Appendix

THE PISTE AND THE CONDUCT OF THE BOUT

The area on which fencing bouts are fought is called a piste or strip. The piste is 14 metres long and from 1·80 to 2 metres wide. There is a centre line, drawn across the middle of the piste. Two metres either side of this line another line is drawn – the on guard line. Another line, the warning line, is drawn 1 or 2 metres from the ends of the piste, depending on the weapon being fought: 1 metre from the end of the piste at foil and 2 metres from each end at sabre and épée.

The bout is conducted by a referee (the president). The referee stands on the side but outside the piste. The first fencer called to the piste by the scorer goes to the on guard line to the referee's right and the other takes the position on his left. They come on guard with their front foot just behind the on guard line so they are out of contact with one another. The referee will maintain his posi-tion by moving backwards and forwards with the fencers' movements.

The bout is started by the referee asking both fencers if they are ready. On the affirmative, he will say 'Play', upon which the bout commences and the fencers will not stop until the referee calls 'Halt'.

Two judges positioned behind each fencer decide the validity of the hits. Alternatively, the hits are recorded by an electrical record-ing apparatus, which signals a valid hit by a coloured light and a non-valid hit by a white light, at the same time sounding a buzzer or bell. Most competitions, except those for very young children, are monitored by elec-tric apparatus.

A loaded spool at each end of the piste allows a wire attached to each fencer to be paid out or wound in as the fencers move backwards and forwards. The spool is connected by cable to the electric recording apparatus situated to one side of the centre of the piste. This apparatus has clearly visible

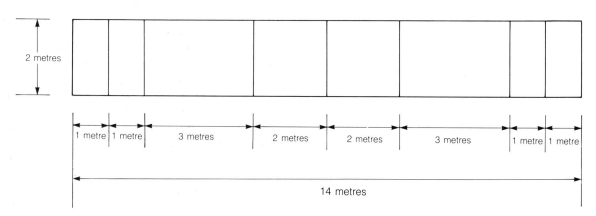

Fig 112   The combat area – the dimensions and markings of the piste.

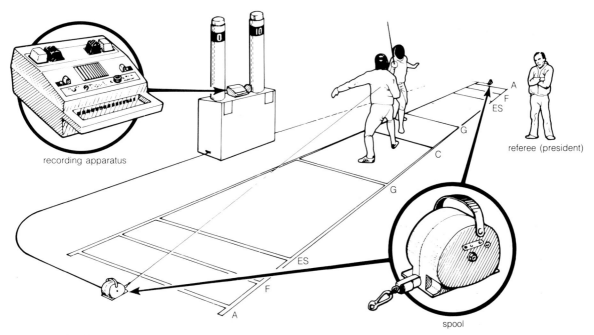

Fig 113 The electric ground equipment and the position of the referee (the president).

lights, a green and a white on one side and a red and a white on the other. The coloured lights register valid hits and the white lights indicate non-valid hits. Each fencer wears an over jacket which just covers the target area and has a metal thread woven into it so that when a foil tip makes contact the coloured light will register the hit. Each fencer has a body wire, which is attached to the spool wire at his back. The wire runs down his sword-arm sleeve and into a socket inside the guard of his weapon.

At épée only the coloured lights are required since the whole of the target is valid. The circuit is therefore simpler and metal jackets are not required.

The piste is covered by a metal surface which, when hit, earths out the circuit and so doesn't register.

During the past few years experiments have been made to introduce electric recording apparatus for sabre similar to that used for épée and foil. All sorts of problems had

to be overcome due to the extended target, and the fact that there is no button on the sabre; point hits must register, and in addition it must be possible for cuts, but not beats, to be recorded.

Experiments have been carried out with a system that requires a lamé jacket covering the valid target, including the arms, and a mask which will make an electrical contact through the jacket circuit. This latter is achieved by means of a wire which clips on to the mask and also makes contact with the jacket. The sabre itself has only been modified by the insertion of a trip-switch inside the guard, and, of course, an inside guard socket to make provision for a body-wire, similar to that worn for foil.

The sabre circuit is made simpler as hits can only be scored when the blade comes into contact with the jacket or mask, in other words, with the electrical conducting surface. Before the hit can actually be registered on the recording apparatus, the trip-switch (which acts as a sensor) must be activated by a cut and this cut must happen at precisely the time the contact is made and not fractions of a second after. This means that, if you make a beat on the blade and then hit flat with your attack, it will not register. The same applies with a point hit, and certain difficulties are experienced when making this type of hit into an opponent's running or flèching attack – if he just runs on to the end of the point, your hit will not register, even though you may have the right of way according to the rules. In order for the point to register, it must be travelling forward.

Any hits arriving on the non-valid surface will not register at all so it is essential that sabre fencers continue all their phrases and do not stop until the president actually calls 'Halt'. It is very easy, once you have felt yourself hit your opponent, to relax and be hit, only to find your own hit has not registered.

The application of the rules is the responsibility of the referee and his judgment of time is final. His authority covers the fencers, team managers, officials and even the audience around the piste.

The two fencers have the use of the whole piste, but although they move backwards and forwards as much and as fast as they wish they must not step off the piste with both feet. If they do go off the side of the piste they will lose a metre of ground and if they step off the end of the piste with both feet, they will first be given a warning and will be placed on guard on the metre warning line. If following the warning, they go off the rear limit of the piste with both feet without having advanced to the centre of the piste with the front foot, with no further warning they will be penalised by a hit.

The bout will be stopped every time a hit is made. If it is a good hit (on target and in time), the president will award a point to the fencer who made the hit. This point must be written down on the score sheet at the time it is awarded. The two fencers are then put on guard behind their on guard line and the bout is re-started. If a point is not awarded, the two fencers are put on guard where they are on the piste and if this means they are too close, they must both give way. Whenever possible the president will be assisted by a scorer and a timekeeper. The scorer's duty is to keep the official score sheet and read out the order of fights. The timekeeper's duty is to record the actual fencing time, stopping the clock every time the referee calls 'Halt' and re-starting it on the command 'Play' and to warn the referee when there is only one minute of fencing time left. It is the timekeeper's duty to stop the bout when time has expired. At the end of the bout at foil and sabre if two fencers are equal on hits, they are allowed as much time as is necessary for one of them to score the decider.

Fencers in a competition are usually divided up into equal groups, called pools, usually of 5 or 6. Each pool is fenced to its conclusion, with each fencer meeting each of the others. At least half of the fencers in the pool (those with the highest scores) are promoted to the next round, the others being eliminated. It is usual to fence to 5 hits with a time limit of 6 minutes.

Another system is direct elimination – a knock-out competition. In the first round the highest seeds fight the lowest seeds – first to 10 hits for men, to 8 hits for ladies. The loser is eliminated and the winner goes through to the next round. Variations of both these systems are also used.

Glossary

AFA Amateur Fencing Association.

Aids The three fingers which help to balance the weapon.

Appel A beat of the foot.

Ballestra A method of delivering an attack by a jump appel.

Beat A preparation of attack by attack on the blade.

Bind A preparation of attack by taking of the blade diagonally from high to low or low to high line.

Body wire The wire that connects a fencer's weapon to the spool wire. The body wire is worn under the jacket going down the sword arm sleeve and out of the back of the jacket.

Bout One single fight.

Breaking ground Retreating.

Break time To change the rhythm of an action by losing time.

Cadence The rhythm.

Ceding parries A defence against prises de fer.

Change of engagement Passing from one engagement to another by passing under the opponent's blade.

Compound offensive action An offensive action including one or more feints.

Compound preparations Preparations executed as one, without interruption.

Coulé An offensive action made by a graze down the opponent's blade.

Counter-attack An offensive action into an offensive action.

Counter-disengagement An offensive action made by deceiving the opponent's change of engagement.

Counter parry Another name for a circular parry.

Counter-riposte A riposte made after the successful parry of a riposte.

Counter-time Any action made by an attacker on his opponent's attempt to stop hit.

Coupé Another name for a cut-over.

Covered position When the way is closed to a direct attack.

Croisé A preparation of attack made by a taking of the blade from the high line to the low line or from low line to the high line on the same side.

Cross-over A type of footwork made by crossing the feet.

Cut To hit with the edge or side of the sabre blade in order to score.

Cut-over A simple attack made by passing the attacking blade over the opponent's.

Dérobement The evasion of the opponent's attempt to beat or take the blade.

Detachment When the blades are not in contact.

Development The lunge.

Direct elimination A method of running a competition. Two fencers fight a bout, the loser of which is eliminated from the competition.

Directoire Technique The committee responsible for organising a competition.

Disengagement A simple attack made by passing the attacking blade under the opponent's.

Double Hit When by a fault two hits arrive at the same time.

Double preparations When the preparations are done in succession with a break.

Engagement When the swords are in contact.

Envelopment A form of preparation by taking of the blade finishing in the line of the original engagement.

False attack An attack which is not intended to hit but to cause a reaction.

137

Feint attack A form of false attack which is not usually complete in itself but deceives the opponent into thinking otherwise.

Fencing measure The distance at which you can just reach your opponent with a lunge.

Fencing time The time it takes to execute one movement of fencing.

FIE Fédération Internationale d'Escrime (International Fencing Federation)

Flèche A method of delivering an attack.

Foible The weakest part of the blade, nearest the tip.

Forte The strongest part of the blade, nearest the guard.

French grip A straight sword handle.

Froissement A preparation of attack by attack on the blade. It is a beat and pressure combined.

Hit To strike the target with the point in order to score. The score is counted on the score sheet in hits for and hits against.

Judge A member of the jury who assists the president to recognise valid or non-valid hits, when fencing is with non-electric weapons, or, in the case of an arm or floor judge, to claim hits on these surfaces.

Line of fence An imaginary line which passes through the heels of both fencers.

Lunge A method of delivering an attack.

Making ground Advancing.

Martingale A loop attached to the sword.

Offensive actions Any action made with the intention of hitting your opponent, such as an attack, a riposte, a stop hit, or a renewal of attack.

On guard The ready position adopted before the word 'play'.

Opposition Resisting the opponent's blade.

Opposition of forte to foible The principle of defence.

Opposition parry Holding and resisting the blade whilst parrying.

Orthopaedic grip A shaped grip which gives better leverage than the straight, or French, grip.

Parry A deflection of the attacking blade with the sword.

Piste The specially marked out area on which a bout is fought.

Pool A group of seeded fencers all of whom fence each other to decide who is promoted to the next round. Pools are usually made up of six fencers.

Pommel The balancing weight at the end of the grip.

Preparation of offensive action A movement which does not in itself hit but causes some reaction from the opponent.

President The president of the jury (referee) is the arbiter of the bout.

Pressure A preparation by attack on the blade. As the name implies, it is a sharp push on the blade.

Principle of défence The opposition of forte against foible in defence.

Priorité de la ligne Priority of the line. This exists when a fencer has the arm straight threatening the opponent's target. The priority is lost if the blade is parried or beaten out of line.

Priority At foil and sabre, the first person to start straightening his arm, point threatening target, has priority until his blade is parried or beaten out of line.

Prise de fer A taking of the blade: the engagement, bind, croisé and envelopment.

Progressive attack An attack of more than one movement executed in one period of fencing time.

Pronated With the palm downwards.

Redoublement A renewal of attack by blade or arm movement.

Referee The president.

Remise A renewal of attack in the same line.

Repêchage In direct elimination competitions, repêchage allows those fencers who have lost their first fight to fight one of the other losers before being eliminated from the competition.

Reprise A renewal of attack passing through the on guard position.

Riposte The offensive action after a successful parry.

Second intention A premeditated action made on an induced response.

Semicircular parry A parry that describes a semicircle.

Simple attack An attack of one blade movement.

Simultaneous action When two fencers simultaneously conceive and execute an action. At foil and sabre no hit is awarded.

Stance Position of the feet when on guard.

Stop hit A counter-attack made by attacking into an attack.

Stop hit in opposition When a stop hit deflects the opponent's blade.

Supinated With the palm upwards.

Three-quarter supinated The usual position in fencing, with the palm upwards and the thumb slightly to the side.

Taking of the blade A prise de fer.

Trompement Deceiving an opponent's parry.

Index